D1592827

To my family, community and friends, who have made this work possible.

CHRIST
AND THE UNIVERSE

Teilhard de Chardin and the Cosmos

by Robert Hale O.S.B. Cam.
edited by Michael Meilach O.F.M.

FRANCISCAN HERALD PRESS

1434 W. 51st St. Chicago, Ill. 60609

Christ and the Universe: Teilhard de Chardin and the Cosmos by Robert Hale O.S.B. Cam., edited by Michael Meilach O.F.M. Copyright 1973 by Franciscan Herald Press, 1434 West 51st Street, Chicago, Illinois 60609. Library of Congress Catalog Card Number: 72-13782. Made in the United States of America.

NIHIL OBSTAT QUOMINUS IMPRIMATUR:
  Benedictus Calati, Cam. O.S.B.
  Prior Generalis Camaldulensium O.S.B.
Camalduli, die 10 Nov. 1972

Library of Congress Cataloging in Publication Data

Hale, Robert

  Christ and the universe.

  Based on the author's thesis
  Includes bibliographical references.
  1. Jesus Christ — History of doctrines — 20th century.
2. Teilhard de Chardin, Pierre. I. Title.
BT198.H34   1973   232'.09'04   72-13782
ISBN 0-8199-0449-X

CONTENTS

PREFACE

"What makes us so different from earlier generations," Teilhard remarked in 1943, "and so much more demanding, is the awakening of our consciousness to a new setting that is cosmic in dimensions."[1] The new cosmic experience is indeed overwhelming. When we hear that our own sun is but one among a hundred billion stars gathered into the larger cluster of the galaxy, that these stars are separated from one another by an average distance of about thirty trillion miles, and that our own galaxy is but one among billions, such affirmations by our most trusted scientists simply stagger our imaginations.[2]

The modern theories concerning the nature and the "shape" of the universe are equally unfathomable to most of us.[3] The irony of our quest for understanding is that "as concepts merge and fundamental laws assume increasingly simpler form, the evolving picture becomes ever more remote from experience."[4] We may try to reassure ourselves that, even if most of us laymen can not grasp the nature of our world, at least the scientists among us must be able to form a satisfactory picture of it all. It was Albert Einstein, however, who wrote that

> the most beautiful and most profound emotion we can experience is the sensation of the mystical. . . . He to whom this emotion is a stranger, who can no longer wonder and stand rapt in awe, is as good as dead. To know that what is impenetrable to us really exists, manifesting itself as the highest wisdom and the most radiant beauty which our dull faculties can comprehend only in their most primitive forms — this knowledge, this feeling is at the center of true religiousness.[5]

We tend to focus on the spatial aspect of this mystery, on the vast dimensions opened up by telescope and microscope.

But scientists remind us that we must add the dimension of time, and again the new universe confronting our consciousness leaves us astonished and awed. Our galaxy is now believed to be about ten billion years old, and our earth roughly half that age. Man is seen to be very much the "late-comer,"[6] awed as much by the temporal as by the spatial enormity of his world.

Now, Teilhard insists that evolution furnishes a key to this universal immensity — a context that brings to our task a real coherence and reestablishes man's own cosmic significance. Thanks to the basic evolutionary insight, we can articulate a new vision of the universe.

> Henceforth the Universe assumes an additional dimension for our experience. It has ceased to be the formal garden from which we are temporarily banished by a whim of the Creator. It has become the great work in process of completion . . . a cosmogenesis.[7]

But a new vision of the universe necessitates the reformulation of theology; Teilhard's own life-work was born of the "conviction of the necessity for the Church to present dogma in a more real, more universal way — a more 'cosmogonic' way."[8]

Most theologians would acknowledge with Butterworth that "there is urgent need for a new theological appreciation of creation in Christian theology."[9] The anthropotropic method of contemporary theology requires a cosmology, and the ecological challenge, which asks nothing less than whether our world can survive, renders this requirement all the more crucial. In the past Christians have sometimes thought of creation as simply a resource to be exploited. But if (as Teilhard argues) the universe is to be understood as intrinsically Christic, then there should be a much more reverential attitude toward it. Man must come to affirm with Teilhard: "I can be saved only by becoming one with the universe."[10] Teilhard's affirmation of the Christic character of the universe converges also with the theological rediscovery that creation is not a mere philosophical theory, but a specifically Christian mystery — a truth which "must have its place in the revelation of God which is Christ our Lord."[11]

The universe is, then, a crucial issue for the Christianity of our day, an issue to which Teilhard has an important contribution to make. The very clarity of all the recent work done on Teilhard's Christology may, however, have obscured his equally fundamental, closely related theological interest in the universe.[12] This book may be seen as an effort to remedy that situation. It will study Teilhard's theology of the universe in the light of his key model, the cosmic Body of Christ, and in the complementary light of his chief speculative affirmation that the universe is intrinsically Christic.

Teilhard's theology of the universe is illumined in a special way by his boldest and most suggestive model, that of Christ's cosmic Body. Although this model has been analyzed with great competence in terms of its Christological implications, little attention has been paid to its more direct and literal import—that the universe *is Christ's Body*—and what this implies for a theology of the universe. Of course Christology and theological cosmology are intimately related in Teilhard, but if Wildiers is right, that the universe was the "primary and major theme on which Teilhard deliberated," then we should be able more easily to penetrate to the core of his vision by pursuing specifically his thought on the Christic universe, rather than considering his vision primarily in terms of Christological questions that he approached, for the most part, only obliquely.

Studies of Teilhard's concept of the total Christ have demonstrated that the French mystic conceived of the entire universe as, at the very least, somehow under the dominion or lordship of Christ. But it constitutes an additional, decisive step to argue that the universe relates to Christ not merely as an extrinsic possession but somehow as intrinsic element, as his *Body*. A whole spectrum of possible positions stretches out in this area.

1. Jesus is only an individual man, and to speak of his "Body" encompassing other persons or the universe simply betrays that kind of mythological thinking which must be purged from the kerygma.

2. Through grace the soul is rendered Christlike and may thus be metaphorically described as pertaining to Christ's "Body." But since the soul is substantial form of its body, the

body too is described by extension of the metaphor as a "member of Christ's Body." But since grace does not inhere in subhuman creatures, one cannot speak of them as encompassed in that Body.

3. Although creatures other than humans may not be said to belong to Christ's "Body," he does exercise a certain headship of authority over the universe, which has an eternal destiny as a kind of context for the elect's life of glory.

4. Christ is Head of the universe in sense significantly more literal than a simple "overlordship" of authority, and the cosmos is mysteriously inserted into the total Christ, the glorified Body of Christ — but in a way subordinate to the elect's participation in the Lord's Body.

It will be maintained in this study that Teilhard held the fourth of these positions, expressed in his central model of Christ's cosmic Body and articulated in a sustained, speculative way throughout his writings. Our essay is thus foundational in nature, arguing the presence and prevalence of this affirmation in Teilhard. The hope is that what cannot be accomplished within its necessarily limited scope, will be undertaken by others: viz., the exploration of all the rich consequences flowing from the vision of the universe as Christ's Body.[13]

Since it is a model we shall be studying all through the book, it is important to begin with an explanation of the theological model as a basic tool. We do so in Chapter One, not so as to impose a foreign framework on Teilhard's thought (he was acquainted with the language of models), but rather to bring to explicit awareness the various key elements involved in his use of models.

Teilhard's intuition regarding the cosmic Body of Christ, which is articulated with particular vividness in his early writings (analyzed in Chapter Two), was nourished throughout his life by his ever deepening contact with scripture and tradition and by the encouragement of some fellow scholars. He often insisted that his thought should be considered not in isolation, as pure innovation, but rather in the context of this rich heritage, which we shall discuss, somewhat briefly of necessity, in Chapter Three, where our main purpose will be trace the broader theological context needed to understand and vindicate Teilhard's outlook.

Teilhard's more experiential, concrete model of Christ's cosmic Body was complemented and spelled out through a more speculative articulation of the universe as an organic whole which is intrinsically, constitutively Christic. This more speculative articulation of his vision is analyzed in Chapters Four and Five. It is important to notice this double level: a theological articulation is surely enriched when it has recourse to both concrete model and speculative formulation. What the latter provides in terms of nuanced, systematic analysis, the former complements with vividness and depth, and the capacity to evoke a profounder insight.

A special debt of gratitude is due to Dr. Ewert Cousins, Father George Maloney, S.J., and Father Robert Gleason, S.J., for their invaluable contributions to the development and completion of the doctoral dissertation on which the present volume is based.

CHAPTER ONE
Cosmic Insight and Model

One of the characteristic notes of Teilhard's writings is the startling, original quality of his terminology. Biogenesis, cephalization, Christogenesis, corpusculization, cosmogenesis —remarkable and problematic neologisms such as these punctuate the pages of his essays. Many of them draw their inspiration from the biological sciences,[1] and among these the phrase "cosmic Body of Christ" certainly stands as one of the most remarkable, startling for both the speculative theologian and the common-sense empiricist.

Is the Body of Christ not a totally supernatural reality, the theologian might inquire, and is it not by grace that we are incorporated into it? And one hardly thinks of planets and other elements of the sub-human realm as endowed with sanctifying grace.[2] Besides, should the mystical Body of Christ not be equated specifically with the Catholic Church?[3] How, then, can the category be expanded to encompass not only other non-Catholics and non-Christians, but even subhuman creatures?

The empiricist, it seems, would be equally startled by what he would doubtless regard as a particularly odd and dubious sort of discourse. How could one verify such a notion? In what direction would one point the telescope to catch a glimpse of the cosmic countenance?

However unusual the phrase might seem to common sense, the Oxford theologian Ian T. Ramsey reminds us that the religious sphere is precisely of such a unique and mysterious nature that "we must expect religious language to be appropriately odd, and to have a distinctive logical behaviour. Otherwise it would not be currency for the strange kind of situation about which it claims to speak."[4]

1

Thus if Teilhard's language seems inappropriate to his critics, the problem might lie largely with their own way of
approaching his writings — with their method of interpreting
his language. The theologian must find a methodology which
respects the special character of such language and illumines
its religious matrix and forms. The model methodology, to
which science has had such fruitful recourse, provides a rich
possibility for theology as well:

> . . . both theology and science are concerned in their own way with the
> disclosure of a mystery. Because of the vastness, complexity, and
> depth of the physical universe and the limits of the human mind, it is
> appropriate for the scientist to use models. In that way he can obtain
> some knowledge, but only part of the whole. The same can be said for
> theological concepts and symbols. Theology is concerned with the
> ultimate level of religious mystery, which is even more inaccessible
> than the mystery of the physical universe. Hence our religious lan-
> guage and symbols should be looked upon as models because, even
> more than the concepts of science, they only approximate the object
> they are reflecting.[5]

The similarity between the use of models in physical science
and in theology should not be exaggerated,[6] true, but the
method clearly does bridge the two areas, and one cannot
help reflecting how congenial this is to Teilhardian thought. A
basic characteristic of Teilhard's language, as already noted,
is its application of biological categories to theology to evoke
religious, cosmic insight. Teilhard, moreover, was thoroughly
at home with the language of the model methodology. He
speaks, e.g., of "constructing models of God,"[7] of the "mechanical model of the World,"[8] and of the need for "some
visible model" for his analysis of "the synthesizing power of
love over the inner life."[9]

Teilhard is, of course, primarily a religious thinker. In
seeking to interpret him, therefore, we "have to go back to an
initial intuition that unremitting thought can never exhaust
or fully express."[10] His thought can never be abstracted from
his own "highly personal spiritual experience,"[11] and the
model method both respects and illumines that cosmic,
Christic intuition that constitutes the heart and matrix of his
thought.[12]

"BODY" AS A MODEL

The basic idea behind the use of models is familiar: one has recourse to a more manageable reality to illumine some aspect of a less manageable one. It is not easy, e.g., to deal with the total mystery of Christ; but we are quite familiar with the notion of shepherd or door, and through these more accessible models (even when they are not taken pictorially) we can gain a truly fruitful insight into the larger mystery.

> Jesus did not go about Palestine leading sheep from place to place; nor did he protect the entrance to a house. . . . [But] he was not, in using these models, failing to describe his own nature and function. He was, in fact, describing his own nature and saying that he could be trusted as a leader. . . . He was saying that it was his purpose to open the way for men to come to the Father. . . .[13]

Thus the model, even when not taken pictorially — indeed, precisely because not interpreted pictorially, can make possible a penetrating articulation of a mystery. Like "door" or "shepherd," the model term should usually be "a down-to-earth word . . . having a plain straightforward use in relation to ordinary situations."[14] For obviously if the model is as obscure and remote as the difficult reality it is meant to help clarify, it is of little value for clarification. A model should be a thing or situation "with which we are all familiar, and which can be used for reaching another situation with which we are not so familiar."[15]

It is immediately evident that Teilhard's model of "Body" admirably fulfills this first requirement of accessibility. As Splett observes, "the body is the most immediate and proximate object of our experience. It is always with us, inseparable from us."[16] Of course the human body, because of its union with personhood, constitutes a quite unique reality: "The body is not merely an object with which man is confronted, it is something which he himself *is:* the pleasure and pain of the body are his own pleasure and pain."[17]

We thus realize that in treating of the Body of Christ we are, in a mysterious manner, talking about Christ himself. And so the model of Body, though accessible, concrete, familiar, and "down-to-earth," is nevertheless in no way a closed or constricted category; rather, it directly leads into the mysterious dimension of human (and divine) personhood. Moreover, it opens out into yet another vast dimension, that of the cosmic or universal: "The world too is not just opposed to the body as the space outside it: it is rather its and hence our 'extension,' and is only there insofar as it is seen, heard, and so on—down to the atmosphere which is our breath."[18]

The notion of the body as that which, rather than partitioning man off from the universe, actually binds him to the whole of creation, is a key concept very central to the biblical vision, as we shall note later. It is also a theme stressed by Teilhard:

> My own body is not these cells or those cells that belong exclusively to me: it is what, in these cells and in the rest of the World feels my influence and reacts against me. My matter is not a part of the Universe that I possess *totaliter:* it is the totality of the Universe possessed by me *partialiter.*[19]

Thus we see the extraordinary richness and depth of Teilhard's "Body" model which, on the one hand, opens into the entire universe, and, on the other, leads into the very personhood of Christ. The cosmic and the Christic are consequently brought into fecund contact at the point of "Body," and this fruitful contact demonstrates the success of Teilhard's model. Like every successful model, it

> involves the juxtaposition and consequent interpenetration of two contexts in such a way as to produce fresh disclosure which includes both within itself. . . [so that] discourse concerning one is facilitated and enriched through the application to it of the terms of discourse of the other.[20]

Nor is this fruitful conjunction of Christic and cosmic forced by rhetoric and argument.[21] It results rather from the intrinsic logic of the model "Body" and its qualifiers "cosmic" and "Christ's." The theme of Christ's Body necessarily leads into that of Christ's own personhood because his Body is in strictest union with his Person. And Teilhard must consider the entire cosmic dimension in which that Body is rooted because "in him all things were created in heaven and on earth, visible and invisible" (Col. 1:16).

Given this richness and depth of the "Body" model—its

organic and synthesizing character—one easily understands
how it became a "dominant model" for Teilhard in his endeavor to work out a theology of the universe.[22] For the various
models in the writings of a thinker rarely stand in simple
juxtaposition. In theology, "the model which sets the phenomena of scripture and of the life of faith . . . within the
deepest perspective tends to gain ascendancy."[23] But breadth
as well as depth of perspective determines the primary model:
"One model is more dominant than another when it pre-
sides . . . over a greater range of discourse."[24] But in depth
and breadth this "relationship of Christ to the whole of creation provides the key"[25] to Teilhard's thought:

> [O God,] let others, fulfilling a function more august than mine, pro-
> claim your splendours as pure spirit; as for me, dominated as I am by
> a vocation which springs from the inmost fibres of my being, I have no
> desire, I have no ability, to proclaim anything except the innumerable
> prolongations of your incarnate Being in the world of matter; I can
> preach only the mystery of your Flesh, O Soul which shines through
> all that surrounds us.[26]

If "the bond of Christ with the universe through the mediation of his Incarnation" constitutes "the key intuition of Teilhard,"[27] the "cosmic Body of Christ" is going to provide the
broadest and most penetrating model for the articulation of
that Christic-cosmic conjunction. This model not only pre-
sides, it integrates. Regarding this integrative function of
models, McIntyre writes that

> by their presence in christological formulation, they provide it with a
> unity which it did not have when theologians did not rely so heavily as
> they do today on models as controlling categories. . . . Theology [to-
> day] is highly integrated and carefully structured, and the medium of
> articulation is the theological model.[28]

This integrative effect is very likely due to the fact that the
models are rooted in mystery and allow the theologian to
articulate his thought always in terms of the reference and
norm of that mystery.[29] The very notion of unity is itself a
model,[30] which is decisive for Teilhard in his articulation of a
theology of the universe as organized whole.[31]

From Ramsey and McIntyre we learn of two criteria according to which the theological model should be judged. The

first, already alluded to above, is "its stability over the widest possible range of phenomena . . . its ability to incorporate the most diverse phenomena not inconsistently."[32] But it was precisely because Teilhard needed a model capable of incorporating a range of phenomena cosmic in scope that he proposed the model of Christ's cosmic Body, which will be seen, as we proceed, to be immeasurably fruitful.

The second criterion is the stimulus offered by the model toward deep commitment and constructive action. The preferable model is the one which "sustains faith and renews it with the very life of Christ," which "leads to fresh commitment to him for work to be done in his name and for his kingdom's sake."[33] But it is well known how totally Teilhard's life was committed to re-inspiring lethargic Christians to action—to real commitment, to the task of building the earth.[34] The entire first part of *The Divine Milieu,* for example, is devoted to the theme of "the divinization of our activities."[35] Notice how Teilhard finds hope and motivation for human endeavor precisely in the model of Christ's cosmic Body:

> O Lord, repeat to me the great liberating words, the words which at once reveal and are operative: *Hoc est Corpus meum.* . . . The things in our life which terrify us . . . are, ultimately, only the matter and species of the one Sacrament.[36]

Teilhard once described his own vocation as a call "to reach heaven by bringing earth to perfection. To Christify matter. There is the whole adventure of my life."[37] We see, then, that Teilhard's key model of cosmic Body of Christ is not just an abstract formula proposed to fill some slot in a speculative system; rather it constitutes a key motivation to hope and commitment which transforms his entire life into adventure.

ONLY A MODEL?

It is evident that many elements of the model methodology help illumine and articulate what Teilhard means in proposing his vision of the cosmic Body of Christ. Still, this vision is such a central and compelling reality for him that we must ask whether it is adequately treated in terms of the category "model."

McIntyre argues that the theory of models updates the doctrine of analogy, makes it useful for theology today, and serves as its foundation.[38] Ramsey, however, rejects analogy and links his notion of model to metaphor instead.[39] It is worth emphasizing, therefore, that Teilhard understands his category "cosmic Body of Christ" to be much more than mere metaphor. He always interprets the phrase in a thoroughly realistic manner, and he insists that such realism is the heritage of scripture and tradition:

> Minds that are afraid of a bold concept or are governed by individualistic prejudices and always try to interpret the relations between beings as moral and logical are quite content to think of the Body of Christ by analogy with aggregates of men. For them it is much more like a social assembly than a natural organism. Such minds dangerously weaken scripture and make it unintelligible or platitudinous to thinking men who are eager to trace out physical interconnections and relations that are specifically cosmic. They unjustifiably diminish Christ and the profoundly real mystery of his Flesh. No, the Body of Christ is not, as some unenterprising thinkers would have us believe, the extrinsic or juridical association of men who are embraced by one and the same benevolence and are destined to the same reward. It must be understood with boldness, as St. John and St. Paul and the Fathers saw it and loved it. It constitutes a World which is natural and new, an organism which is animate and in motion, one in which we are all united, physically and biologically.[40]

One must, then, "be chary of speaking of 'the metaphor' of the Body of Christ":

> It is almost impossible to exaggerate the materialism and crudity of Paul's doctrine of the Church as literally now the resurrection body of Christ. . . . The body that he has in mind is as concrete and as singular as the body of the Incarnation.[41]

And for theologians like McIntyre, who link model with analogy rather than metaphor, it would be a gross falsification to think of a model as merely a kind of mask which conceals, and which need only be stripped away in order to attain the reality itself. Rather, a model is precisely the means for getting to deeper reality. The whole point of analogy, as opposed to metaphor, is that the term used analogously does apply literally to the reality.

Most Catholic theologians hold that we can never presume to treat of the transcendent, ineffable God in the immediacy of non-analogical language. But is the situation not somewhat altered when we approach the subject of Jesus Christ—the God-*man?* Even McIntyre, who so stresses the analogical character of models, argues that some language about Christ penetrates beyond the level of model—e.g., truth, *logos.* There is, McIntyre insists, "an identity of content between them and the very nature of Christ which precludes the rough approximations of model-type assertions."[42]

When the *Bhagavad-Gita* speaks of the "body of God," a Western theologian would have to say that "body" is being referred to God metaphorically; but when one speaks of the body of Christ the matter is certainly more intricate and nuanced. For Jesus of Nazareth did in fact possess a mortal body (*was* a body, the Hebrew mind would affirm). By faith, moreover, we believe in the resurrection of that body. We believe that Christ's body still exists. And we believe that the body, because glorified, possesses certain mysterious dimensions which many theologians call "cosmic." So when Teilhard refers to the Body of Christ, he means to talk specifically and directly about Christ's body and not about something else. The term is not figurative or metaphorical, but quite literal.

Of course when Teilhard uses the term "Body," he and his readers must recur to the image of the earthly, unglorified human body to give the term content. Still, the reference is not to that earthly body, but to Christ's glorified Body, so that there is not a simple "one-one" correspondence between the usual earthly meaning of the word and its mysterious referent in glory. The special difficulty caused by this lack of easy correspondence is discussed in the section immediately following.

THE QUALIFIERS

A further fruitful characteristic of the model method is that it spells out the significant function of qualifiers in religious language. Theologians who utilize the method note that religious models tend to be modified by qualifying terms which thrust the meaning radically beyond the normal connotations of the model. Thus God is not simply wise, he is *infinitely* wise; he is not only powerful, but *all*-powerful; he is not only cause, but *first* cause. Theology thus provides "built-in stimuli" for the indefinite development of a model, and the development is done by the addition of "qualifiers" that spell out particular aspects of the model as it applies to the reality being described.[43]

Now, it is most significant that Teilhard always carefully qualifies his category of "Body" by indicating that he is treating precisely of *Christ's* Body, of Christ's *glorified* Body, and of Christ's glorified Body in its *cosmic* dimension.

It is always clear, first that Teilhard is treating of Christ's Body rather than some mere metaphorical body or divine presence, some moral body of humans, or the totality of creation as a collectivity.[44] Teilhard's thought is always decisively Christocentric and realist, reflecting his interior religious experience and its focus from the time of his youth.[45]

Teilhard refers, moreover, to Christ's glorified Body rather than to that body in its earthly state; his discussion of Christ's cosmic Body is indissolubly linked to the mystery of the Resurrection.[46] But a problem arises regarding his "realistic" understanding of "Body of Christ." We have noted Teilhard's vivid sense of Christ's glorified Body and the "physical bonds" that link it with the rest of creation. But now we see that Teilhard refers to the glorified Body, a fact which may seem to compromise the non-metaphorical realism of his category. For when he uses the category "Body," he must recur to the image of the earthly body of our experience, which does not correspond to the risen Body he wants to discuss.

There are intrinsic linguistic, philosophical, and theological questions involved here, which we cannot consider adequately. We can and must indicate, however, the direction in which theologians see the solution to lie: it is in the continuity between the earthly and the glorified Body. We should not interpret "Body" in a too visually descriptive way, and if this caution is observed, the term does apply strictly to Christ's glorified state. To the extent that the glorified spiritual Body is different from the earthly body, moreover, the model method is ideally suited to safeguard and illumine that difference.[47]

But it is the term "cosmic" that represents Teilhard's most

original qualifier of the "Body" model. A qualifier is expressly designed to make sure that "the main point of the model is seen to be its fulfillment in disclosure."[48] It stimulates continuous development of the model's cosmic scope and profundity. Through careful analysis and creative insight, the theologian brings these qualifiers together, compares them, and combines them so that they disclose more and more strikingly the model they qualify and the reality signified.

Surely Teilhard's qualifier "cosmic" fulfills these functions: it adds dimension and depth to the model of "Body," opening it to the vast religious mystery of the Total Christ. A major objection to the official concept of the mystical Body is that it tended to become a "stiff, all-too-pat model."[49] The theologians of the Roman Curia tended to develop it too speculatively—in "purely juridical categories."[50] Teilhard explodes all this juridical rigidity. By his qualifier of "cosmic" he opens up the model of Christ's Body to a universal extension, a universal import. And it is this profoundly religious mystery of the Total Christ which Teilhard seeks to illumine.

Precisely as cosmic, then, Teilhard's model achieves its special efficacy for religious disclosure. It evokes a deep, inclusive cohesion as it broadens the Christic focus to include all the universe—so that center becomes circumference. This is no coincidence; on the contrary, cosmic disclosure constitutes the real heart of Christian theology. Qualifiers witness to theology's "grounding in permanent mystery," and they point to "a cosmic disclosure as that alone which reveals the topic of any and every theological utterance."[51]

The parallelism between Ramsey's doctrine and Teilhard's vision becomes striking as Ramsey describes religious commitment as "a total commitment to the whole universe." The Christian religion in particular

> focuses such a cosmic commitment on Christ—on Christ as Jesus of Nazareth, born, dead, and buried, but also on the risen and ascended Christ, the cosmic Christ of Ephesians and Colossians, the Christ who is organic to the old Israel and to the new Israel of his Church and through them to the whole of history.[52]

We may conclude, then, that the model-qualifier method is

particularly well suited for interpreting Teilhard's Christic cosmology. By insisting on his central category of Christ's cosmic Body, Teilhard seeks to evoke a cosmic commitment and vision wherein "every particle, every process must, through some part of itself, appear in the definitive reality of Christ. . . . The Universe assumes the form of Christ."[53]

TEILHARD AND COSMIC INSIGHT

The principal asset of the model methodology as applied to Teilhard's thought consists in its clear insistence on the experiential matrix underlying the written expression and on the function of theological and religious language to evoke insight into mystery. To come to terms fully with the discursive level of a theological or religious thinker, one must penetrate to the deeper ground of experiential, religious insight.[54] Hence Teilhard's warning at the outset of a 1950 essay:

> Despite certain appearances of dialectical rigor, the considerations which follow do not seek to develop a learnedly coherent construction, a philosophy of things. They seek, on the contrary, to relate a direct interior experience.[55]

In analyzing Teilhard's model of cosmic Body of Christ, as well as his more technical elaboration of the intrinsically Christic character of the universe which complements the model, we shall always have to bear in mind the deep experiential ground of his articulation.[56] At this point, therefore, we must attempt at least a brief examination of that religious, experiential ground.

This is a task which, because of the profundity of Teilhard's experience, we undertake with a certain diffidence. It is always hard to deal with the interior life of others, but in treating of Teilhard, who has been described as "one of the most unique personalities in the mysticism of Christ"[57] and as "one of the greatest mystics of all time,"[58] we must remain particularly mindful of that difficulty and not aspire to more than a tentative description of some aspects of his rich experience.

The deep, interior interaction of Teilhard's "two loves" has been cited as a key catalyst for his spiritual development as well as for the articulation of his thought:

From the first lines that Teilhard writes the problem is already posed which will occupy the entirety of his life: how to harmonize the love of the World and the love of God. It is posed, not as a theoretical question, but rather as a lived experience.[59]

Thus Teilhard is already writing in 1917 of "the two elements which sum up life for me,"[60] and thirty years later he sums up his life task as

an effort of intellectual reflexion which will establish that the two faiths confronting one another (faith in God and faith in man) are not in opposition to one another: on the contrary, they represent the two essential components of a complete humano-Christian mysticism.[61]

Of course Teilhard came to see these two faiths, these two loves as decisively reconciled, indeed united in the person of the cosmic Christ: "Our Lord Jesus Christ—what else is there besides this synthesis of the created Universe and its Creator?"[62] It is clear how direct is the trajectory from this interior synthesis of the two loves to Teilhard's articulation of his vision in terms of the model of Christ's cosmic Body and his theology of the intrinsically Christic universe.

But Teilhard was not able from the very beginning to achieve this harmonious synthesis of his two loves. Particularly in his early years (and it is extraordinary at what a young age Teilhard began his quest) there were storms and crises. Even in his early period, however, he felt a strong need for a Plenitude, a Center:

The sense of Plenitude: as far back as I go in my infancy, nothing seems more characteristic or more familiar to my interior life than the taste or irresistible need for some "Uniquely Sufficient and Uniquely Necessary Reality."[63]

In those days he sometimes tended to confuse some of matter's more impressive manifestations with the magnetic Presence at its heart:

I was not more than six or seven when I felt myself attracted by matter, or rather by some reality glowing at its core . . . I withdrew into the savored contemplation of my "God of Iron." Yes, Iron. And I can still see, with amazing clarity, my collection of idols . . . I can't help smiling when I recall this attitude of childhood. And yet, at the same time, I must recognize that in this instinctive tendency to adore a piece of metal there are revealed a series of aspirations and an intensity of donation of which my whole spiritual life was but the development.

And why iron . . . if not because, for my immature experience as a child, nothing was heavier, nothing harder, nothing more durable . . . Stability, consistence; that for me was undoubtedly the fundamental attribute of Being.[64]

Teilhard goes on to recount his youthful disillusionment at the discovery that iron rusts. This anxious sense of the contingency of the creation he so loved evolved into his deep concern to find some "way out," some ultimate issue, through which the highest values of the universe could escape the threat of death, of cataclysm. His conviction that the universe could not simply disintegrate was "less the result of a philosophical analysis than of an attraction for the absolute deeply imbedded in his personality":[65]

Cosmic sense and Christic sense: in me two axes apparently independent of each other at birth; yet only after much time and effort did I at last grasp . . . their connection, their convergence, and finally their ultimate identity.[66]

It is easy to see how the key notions of "ground and support" for the universe, issue, plentitude, Christic sense, cosmic sense — all converge in the model of Christ's cosmic Body and in the affirmation of the intrinsically Christic character of creation.

This is not to say, as already noted, that Teilhard immediately and serenely achieved his vision. Rather, there were to be personal crises as the spirituality of the period pressed the young student toward the disjunction rather than the synthesis of his two loves. Speaight notes that

early photographs of Teilhard show him as more serious, or at least more solemn, than he was afterwards to appear. . . . he was suffering from a deep interior division. The normal difficulties of adolescence seem to have passed him by, but it was not easy to reconcile the detachment of the *Imitation* with an increasing attachment to the cosmos. The two absolutes were in conflict. Already at Mongré, he had felt the strain, and he now wondered whether he should not abandon the second for the first. That he did not do so was due to the robust good sense of the 'spiritual father,' Père Paul Troussard, who told him that the crucified Lord was awaiting the natural expansion of his being, no less than its sanctification.[67]

Freed at last by the resolution of this fundamental crisis, Teilhard could pursue without inner torment his "passionate taste for the World." Indeed, his painful encounter with the spirituality of contempt for the world drew the issue sharper for him, and he reacted with a strengthened resolve to proclaim the full Christic destiny of the world:

> There is something deeper in Christianity than an admiration for the Stylites, or the anti-intellectualism of the *Imitation*—and that is its faith in the resurrection of the Earth and the expectation of a consummation of the Universe 'in Christ Jesus.'[68]

By 1919 Teilhard was pursuing fully his scientific interests, and they had a profound impact on his spirit. His work in paleontology, in the field and in the laboratory, the clear accumulation of evidence for an evolutionary process extending billions of years, his close familiarity with the vast, cosmic perspectives of astronomy and the physicist's challenge of entropy: all these factors shaped and refined his full commitment to the universe. As he put it, he was "convinced that there is no more substantial nourishment for the religious life than contact with scientific realities, if they are properly understood."[69] His statements ring with the truth of genuine paradox:

> No one understands so fully as the man who is absorbed in the study of matter, to what a degree Christ, through his Incarnation, is interior to the World. . . . Only that man can fully appreciate the richness contained in the apex . . . who has first gauged the width and the power of the base. . . . By itself, science cannot discover Christ—but Christ satisfies the yearnings that are born in our hearts in the school of science.[70]

It was Teilhard's deep encounter with creation in his scientific labors, then, that spurred on his yearnings for the Center, Animator, and Omega of the universe; and the yearnings were answered through his faith in the cosmic Christ at the heart of matter, illumining matter. Faith instructed him of Christ's presence at the heart of the universe, but by his mystical sense Teilhard was convinced that nature actually nourished him with this presence.

Karl Rahner has portrayed scholasticism's understanding of nature and grace as that of "two layers laid very carefully one on top of the other so that they interpenetrate as little as possible."[71] This description, whether it is fair or not, certainly cannot be applied to Teilhard's vision, That vision of a Christ that is cosmic and a cosmos that is Christic, focuses unerringly on "the Presence . . . behind the blaze of the Universe."[72] In language that would scandalize a Thomas a Kempis, Teilhard exhorts: "Son of man, bathe yourself in the ocean of Matter . . . for it cradled you long ago in your preconscious existence; and it is that ocean that will raise you up to God."[73] This is an extremely rich image, with deep spiritual resonances suggested, e.g., by Mircea Eliade in his study of the primordial image of the "Earth-Mother."[74] Perhaps one of Teilhard's greatest achievements is his reawakening of contemporary Christians—precisely through religious categories—to this realization of their rootedness in matter:

> Where are the roots of our being? In the first place, they plunge back and down into the unfathomable past. How great is the mystery of the first cells which were one day animated by the breath of our souls! How impossible to decipher the welding of the successive influences in which we are for ever incorporated! In each of us, through matter, the whole history of the World is in part reflected. . . .
> The masters of the spiritual life incessantly repeat that God wants only souls . . . the human soul, however independently created our philosophy represents it as being, is inseparable, in its birth and in its growth, from the Universe into which it is born.[75]

One notes here the seminal model of microcosm-macrocosm—we shall encounter it again—as well as the fervent, if delicately worded protest to "the masters of the spiritual life" for their forgetfulness of the religious, sacramental significance of matter. Teilhard writes from his own experience, and so he affirms a creation that is not simply a burden dragging one downward but a means for leverage, an instrument for ascent:

> Imagine a deep-sea diver trying to get back from the seabed to the clear light of day. Or imagine a traveller on a fog-bound mountainside climbing upward toward the summit bathed in light. . . . Both diver and climber can succeed . . . only if they use everything around and about them as points of leverage. . . . Each one of us has his Jacob's ladder, whose rungs are formed of a series of objects. . . .
> Matter, you in whom I find both seduction and strength . . . I

> surrender myself to your mighty layers . . . the virtue of Christ has passed into you. Let your attractions lead me forward, let your sap be the food that nourishes me; let your resistance give me toughness; let your robberies and inroads give me freedom. And finally, let your whole being lead me towards Godhead.[76]

These lines give but a faint taste of their rich and variegated context; but even in what has been cited, the reader will easily discern the depth of Teilhard's cosmic experience: his earnest effort to evoke in others religious insight into the key function of the universe in the spiritual life, in the task of completing the Body of Christ. Fuller discussion of this passage would involve probing the relevance of the patristic image of the ladder to paradise, the patristic theme of the sacramentality of the universe and of the body, and the harmony of Teilhard's vision with both empirical and theological approaches to mysticism in recent times.[77]

None of this can be pursued here, of course, but we can and must stress that Teilhard's spirituality is not simply the nature-mysticism found, e.g., in Horace and Pindar, in Shelley and Wordsworth. Nor can it be reduced to mere pantheism, whatever be the charges of Teilhard's critics and the occasional fear of his friends on this point.[78] Teilhard's is a "mysticism of Christ,"[79] and his entire spirituality is Christocentric, so that he perceives the universe in a specifically Christic form. In his vision

> the universal Christ—the Christ of the Universe, Christ the King, Pantocrator—achieves the synthesis between the cosmic and the Christic, and so, by a stroke of genius, what might have been pantheistic becomes a pan-Christicism . . . [and thus] the Christic function of the Universe—the ascent of the world towards Christ the King with the irresistible surge of the ocean tides under the pull of moon and sun.[80]

The Christic thus binds together Teilhard's cosmic vision as he affirms a "pan-Christism, which, in fact, is simply the notion of the mystical Body, taken in its fullest and most profound sense, and the extension to the Universe of the attributes already accorded . . . to Christ the King."[81] The model of the Body of Christ thus articulates most directly

Teilhard's conception of pan-Christism, his vision of the organic and intrinsically Christic character of the universe.

Given this deep experiential ground of Teilhard's Christic-cosmic vision, we can proceed now to examine its articulation in his model of the cosmic Body of Christ as it occurs in his earliest writings, when, as he himself acknowledges,[82] his vision was at its freshest and most exuberant.

CHAPTER TWO

The Key Early Texts in Teilhard

It may be surprising that Teilhard's early writings should elaborate most fully his difficult theological concept of the universe as Christ's cosmic Body. But it was the young Teilhard who, under the pressure of the tremendous spiritual crisis of his time, felt compelled to resolve the basic issue of the relation between Christ and the universe. A good case can be made that his *Writings in Time of War* contains the essence of his religious thought, expressed often "more clearly, more concisely than in any of his later writings." [1] Certainly his model of the cosmic Body finds its fundamental and fullest explication in the remarkable essays of the war years.

COSMIC LIFE

The first essay to issue from the catalyst of the trenches, *Cosmic Life,* was written in early 1916; Teilhard conceived of it as the "testament of an intellectual," [2] in which he already formulated with great clarity the dilemma of two loves, which he felt constitutes the heart of the modern spiritual crisis. The essay begins:

> There is a communion with God, and a communion with earth, and a communion with God through the earth. . . . I write these lines to express an impassioned vision of the earth, and in an attempt to find a solution for the doubts that beset my action—because I love the Universe, its energies, its secrets, and its hopes, and because at the same time I am dedicated to God, the only Origin, the only Issue, the only Term. I wish these pages to radiate my love of matter and of life, and to harmonize that love, if possible, with the unique adoration of the only absolute and definitive Divinity. [3]

One immediately notes that the essay is characterized not by a dry, detached speculative tone, but rather by the language of deep and personal religious commitment. [4] It is soon evident, as Teilhard continues, that the dilemma of the two loves will find its fundamental resolution in the doctrine of the Body of Christ. This Body he conceives of not in juridical terms, but rather as a physical, organic reality:

> The Body of Christ is not . . . the extrinsic or juridical association of men. . . . [It] must be understood with boldness, as St. John and St. Paul and the Fathers understood it. It constitutes a World that is natural and new, an organism that is animate and in motion, in which we are all united, physically, biologically. . . . At the source of its developments an operation was called for, transcendent in order, to graft the Person of God onto the human cosmos, under conditions that are mysterious but physically governed.[5]

Already, in his first essay of the War Years, Teilhard is proposing his startling terms, "physical" and "biological" to characterize the cosmic interconnections of Christ with "the human cosmos." Clearly the terms are intended to vindicate a realistic conception of God's union with saved creation in Christ.

This first essay also contains one of Teilhard's fullest discussions of the universe as Christ's cosmic Body:

> Jesus Christ by grace is united to all sanctified souls: and since the bonds that link souls to him in one single sanctified mass end in him . . . the whole body is his in its entirety. But souls are not isolated monads. As the "cosmic view" specifically reveals, they make up one single whole with the Universe, consolidated by life and matter. Thus Christ cannot limit his Body to some periphery drawn within things. . . . He can bring souls together and give them life only by assuming with them all the rest of the World. Through his Incarnation he entered not only into mankind but also into the Universe that bears mankind — and this, not only as an element associated with it, but with the dignity and the function of directive principle or center toward which every love and every affinity converge. Mysterious and vast though the mystical Body already be, it does not, accordingly exhaust the immense and salutary integrity of the Word made flesh. Christ has a *cosmic* Body that extends throughout the whole Universe. Such is the final proposition to be borne in mind. "Qui potest capere, capiat."[6]

The central truth Teilhard points to here is not a mere factual datum subject to the usual scientific verification procedure. Indeed, he implicitly admits that the theme is not commonly acknowledged in the theological writings of the time. Rather it represents a difficult mystery, a profound insight for

those capable of glimpsing it: "Qui potest capere, capiat."
Nor does Teilhard regard this as just one theological position
among others; rather this special truth represents for him a
central, organizing principle: "Such is the final proposition to
be borne in mind." In other essays he similarly affirms:

> The entire problem, all my attention, the total attraction of my spiritu-
> al life, have been focused on this point and continue to be focused
> there: how to connect within my person the forces of both these
> centers — God and the World — or, more exactly, how to make them
> coincide.[7]
> This fundamental experience [of Christ as synthesis of the Universe]
> which supports the whole of my spiritual life, may be summed up in
> the following affirmation, which expresses the most basic requirement
> of my interior joy:
>   To be able to admit *a certain* coextension of Christ and the Uni-
> verse so that 1) in Christ is fulfilled the grandeur and power of the
> Universe, and 2) meritorious action can be carried out with the knowl-
> edge that one is thereby acting in union with the whole Universe.
> Behold the only one of my ideas to which I am quite totally com-
> mitted.[8]

At another point in *Cosmic Life* Teilhard stresses the dynamic and incomplete character of the cosmic Christ:

> Since Christ was born, ceased to grow and died, *everything has
> continued in motion because Christ has not yet achieved the fullness
> of his form.* He has not gathered about him the last folds of the
> garment of flesh and love woven for him by his faithful. *The Mystical
> Christ has not attained his full growth — nor therefore has the Cosmic
> Christ.* Of both we may say that they *are* and at the same time *are
> becoming.*[9]

We catch here a first glimpse of the problematic in Teilhard of
the relation between the mystical Christ and the cosmic
Christ. Taken literally the text would suggest we are dealing
with two Christs; but obviously Teilhard is using somewhat
poetic language to describe two dimensions of the Total
Christ. We shall probe at greater length later the exact relation involved.

In the same essay Teilhard proclaims the spiritual, religious import of the cosmic Christ, affirming this theme to be a
"gospel" in which "the salvation of our own times may well
lie," for it resolves modern man's dilemma of the two loves:

There we have the *liberating truth,* the divinely prepared cure for faithful but ardent minds that suffer because they cannot reconcile in themselves two almost equally imperative and vital impulses: faith in the world and faith in God.[10]

CHRIST IN THE WORLD OF MATTER

Later in the same year, 1916, Teilhard mentioned in his correspondence with his cousin a different kind of writing he was working on:

In order to trace a figure as beautiful as I can of our Lord at the heart of things — as I see him in my mind's eye — I thought of something that pleased me greatly. It would consist of three stories in the style of Benson (*The Light Invisible*), three sorts of visions (the Picture, the Monstrance, the Pyx) in which Christ would appear glorified by everything that is blessed in reality and infinitely attainable and active in every creature. . . .[11]

One need not agree with Cuénot that these stories contain "an exact depiction of things Teilhard himself experienced,"[12] to admit that they reflect in a more general way basic intuitions in his experience. *Christ in the World of Matter* is couched in a literary genre rather difficult for the theologian to work with — one that draws from the forms of fiction to express personal religious intuitions. Still, the basic thrust and theological import of the essay are clear.

The "friend" described in the stories, who represents Teilhard himself, formulates the main question: "You want to know . . . how the Universe, in all its power and multiplicity, came to assume for me the figure of Christ?"[13] This experience developed gradually, he explains, through "life-renewing intuition." He cannot imagine Christ's Body merely set beside other bodies, on the same plane of existence:

Confusedly, I found myself saddened and shocked at the idea that the Body of Christ could stand in the midst of a crowd of inferior bodies, in the context of the World, without their sensing and recognizing, by some perceptible alteration, the Intensity so close to them.

As he gazes at a picture of Christ, wondering if the artist has not "imposed on Christ's Body a fixity, a too precise definition," the actual vision begins, its point being that these confining boundaries to Christ are overcome as the cosmic dimension of his Body reveals itself:

> When I allowed my gaze to wander over the outlines of Christ's form, I suddenly became aware that these were *melting away* . . . the folds of his garment, the lustre of his flesh all seemed to merge (though without passing away) into the rest of the picture. It was as though the planes that separated Christ and the surrounding world were melting into a single vibrant surface whereon all demarcations vanished . . . the metamorphosis spread rapidly until it had affected everything.[14]

This first intuition of Christ's cosmic Body is reinforced in the second and third "stories," in which he uses the model of the eucharistic Host in treating of Christ's relation to creation. In the second story the "friend" is again in a church, but now before the Blessed Sacrament exposed in a monstrance. The Host is suddenly seen to expand and encompass everything. This expansion is not a destructive process, for all things are preserved in their unique nature; rather it vivifies in one, translucent flesh:

> The flow of the whiteness enveloped me, passed beyond me, and overran everything. At the same time everything, though drowned in the host, retained its own proper figure, its own autonomous movement; for the whiteness did not efface the features or change the nature of anything, but penetrated objects at the core of their being, at a level more profound than their own life. It was as though a milky brightness were illuminating the Universe from within. All things seemed formed of the same kind of translucent flesh . . . so through the mysterious expansion of the host the World had become incandescent, had itself in its totality become like a single giant Host.[15]

The Universe as consecrated Host: we shall encounter this striking image again later, but here it appears apparently for the first time. It has been carefully explained, with all due distinctions and qualifications, by Teilhard's theological friends, eager to shield him from censure,[16] and it has been attacked fiercely by his critics as, e.g., "simply mythology."[17] Here we wish only to note that the model is not at all marginal in Teilhard, but appears in the context of his central religious question of the relation between Christ and the universe, where it illustrates and buttresses his assertion that the universe is the full extension of Christ's Body.

THE MYSTICAL MILIEU

In an essay written just a few months later, Teilhard seems to suggest it is precisely through the eucharistic action that Christ divinizes all things:

> Since first you said, Lord, "This is my Body," not only the bread of the altar, but (to a certain degree) everything in the universe that nourishes the soul for the life of Spirit and Grace, has become *yours,* become *divine* — it is divinized, divinizing, and divinizable. Every presence makes me feel that you are near me; every contact is the touch of your hand.[18]

Again we note the profoundly religious language regarding the divine (or rather, specifically Christic) presence in all things. The experiential descriptions of his "feel" and "touch" of Christ's presence recall the familiar mystical theme of the "spiritual senses."[19]

The text indicates that the Christification of the universe is not to be understood on the same plane as the eucharistic transubstantiation; nevertheless, it is to be seen in the light of, and as a certain participation in, that sacramental action: "not only the bread of the altar, but (to a certain degree) everything in the Universe. . . . "

Regarding the relation of the mystical to the cosmic Body, Teilhard seems to suggest in one passage of this essay that the categories are almost synonymous: "You have wished, in the mystery of your mystical Body — of your cosmic Body — to feel the echo of every joy and every fear. . . ."[20] The issue is not being treated for its own sake here, but we may perhaps observe that the juxtaposition of the two terms suggests a synonymous function, or perhaps even an expansion and strengthening of "mystical" by "cosmic."

CREATIVE UNION

Another essay toward the end of 1917 develops further the model of cosmic Body. Teilhard, sketching his "philosophy of creative union," observes that "this philosophy is simply the development, the generalization, the extension to the Universe of that which the Church teaches us concerning the growth of Christ."[21] If this theory of creative union provides "perhaps *the* key" to Teilhard's whole vision,[22] it is surely significant for our purposes that this "key" is developed as an extension of the model of Christ's Body: "It is the philosophy of the Universe conceived of in terms of [conçue en fonction de] the notion of the Mystical Body."[23]

Our contention is thus vindicated again, that the texts treating of the cosmic Body are no obiter dicta, but really represent the ground and climax of Teilhard's whole cosmological and theological endeavor. As he himself goes on to say:

> . . . all these reachings-out that draw beings together and unify them constitute the axis of all individual and collective life. It is in virtue of that *axis* that we see that Christ has not only a mystical Body but a *cosmic Body,* the most impressive description of whose chief attributes we owe to St. Paul – even if he never uses the actual term. And this cosmic Body, to be found in all things, and always in process of individualization (spiritualization) is eminently the mystical Milieu. . . . At the term of the creative effort, when the kingdom of God has reached maturity, all the chosen monads and all the elect forces of the Universe will be fused into God through Christ. Then, through the *plenitude* of his individual being, of his mystical Body and his cosmic Body, Christ, in himself alone, will be the heavenly Jerusalem, the new world.

Again the language, interpreted literally, seems to suggest two bodies of Christ: "not only a mystical Body but a *cosmic Body.*"

Can Teilhard's "cosmic Body" be conceived as the *whole,* of which the "mystical Body" represents a part – certainly the pre-eminent part? The wording is open to this interpretation which, whatever other problems it may raise, is surely better than alleging that Teilhard speaks of two distinct, juxtaposed "Bodies." If one tries to explain such a juxtaposition as one Body (persons elevated by grace – mystical Body) next to another (sub-human creatures – cosmic Body), how explain Teilhard's affirmation that "this cosmic Body . . . is eminently the mystical Milieu?" One might expect him to say this of the divine presence, the realm of grace, or even the mystical Body – but he is speaking of the cosmic Body alone. This amazing equation suggests that the cosmic Body has a dignity and significance not at first glimpsed – that it is not enough to conceive of the cosmic Body as just the realm of sub-human creatures metaphorically called "Body" in a forced parallel with the mystical Body.

"Mystical milieu" is, moreover, Teilhard's earlier designation for what he will later term the "divine milieu,"[24] and so his startling equation of these two models is pregnant with significance and must be borne in mind: "This cosmic Body . . . is eminently the mystical Milieu."

MY UNIVERSE

In 1918 Teilhard composed this important essay in which he again proposes Christ as the locus of union of his two loves: "Our Lord Jesus Christ — what else is there besides this synthesis of the created Universe and its Creator?"[25] The concept of two dialectical poles of ultimate significance — God and the universe — finding their one synthesis in Christ reveals how totally Teilhard is committed by his basic vision to the vindication of Christ's real and decisive cosmic significance.

But he is motivated by another concern in affirming the cosmic Christ: viz., a "'faith in the plentitude of Christ." As he goes on to explain, "A Christ who did not sum up in some way, who was not in some way the World itself, such a Christ would seem to me to be too small." His vision of Christ's cosmic Body, far from being a speculative hypothesis, thus emerges as an expression of his inner religious commitment to Christ as his All.

For Teilhard, his admittedly real obligation to give speculative precision to his position holds a "secondary, rather artificial and much more debatable place" relative to the fundamental vision itself. The theologian evaluating that vision must thus bear in mind that he is faced with, literally, a way of seeing and experiencing, primarily, on the religious plane, rather than a speculative system for notional analysis. Some theologians tend to ignore the broader testimony (in poetic and lyrical writing and in informal letters — in one's very life) to the validity of a fundamental vision. We think they are mistaken — they should seek to penetrate beneath speculative formulas to the underlying experience and insight.

In any case, there can be no doubt that "whatever be the

corrections, more or less profound, that must be made,"[26] Teilhard's fundamental challenge to contemporary Christian thought and action, his testimony to his interior vision, will continue to have a broad impact on the Church.

THE PRIEST

The next essay to issue from Teilhard's pen again links the Eucharist with the world in terms of the model of Christ's Body.[27] But in *The Priest* Teilhard employs the image, not simply of the already consecrated Host, but of the entire eucharistic action, from consecration to communion. This essay thus complements *Christ in the World of Matter* just as it heralds the later *Mass on the World,* and we note a remarkable continuity in the development of Teilhard's vision of the total Body of Christ expressed in the image of the Eucharist.

Lacking bread and wine, Teilhard as priest takes the universe itself as his host and chalice: "I shall spread my hands over the whole Universe and take its immensity as the matter of my sacrifice." This action is an expression of the very salvific plan of God which itself extends to the entire universe:

> Is not the infinite circle of things the definitive Host that it is your will to transform?
>
> The seething cauldron in which the activities of all living and cosmic substances are brewed together — is not that the bitter cup that you seek to sanctify?

Anticipating God's definitive transformation of all things, Teilhard resolves to consecrate the whole as Christ's Body:

> I shall look beyond the white host, accepting its domination, and with all the strength of my desire and my prayer, with all my power, over every substance and every development I shall pronounce the words: *Hoc est Corpus meum.*[28]

Now the "divine work is accomplished," and all things are inserted into Christ. But somehow it is the kenotic dimension of Christ:

> Every particle, every process, must, through some part of itself appear in the definitive reality of Christ.
>
> Thus, when I spoke those words, an organic unity, underlying every

substance, was introduced into the isolated elements of nature. Superimposed upon all visible activity, a dominating force now guides individual movements in accordance with a higher plan.

The figure of Christ emerges: it takes on definition in the midst of our nebula of participated beings and secondary causes.

The universe assumes the form of Christ — but O mystery! He whom we discover is Jesus crucified.

The universe constitutes Christ's cosmic Body; but until the Parousia this Body is characterized by a decidedly kenotic quality, a cruciform character. Here we have one of the most significant of Teilhard's observations regarding his model of cosmic Body, which saves his conception from that naive cosmic triumphalism of which many have accused him.

But since the world has been consecrated and is now filled with Christ, there is a real sense in which it, like the earthly body of Christ and the Eucharist, is the object of adoration:

Adoration . . . I kneel, Lord, before the Universe that has imperceptibly, under the influence of the Host, become your adorable Body and your divine Blood.

I prostrate myself in its presence, or better — much better — I recollect myself in that Universe.

The World is filled by you.[29]

In startling language which would scandalize a Barth, we have here the reaffirmation of a universe which, as Christ's Body, constitutes an intrinsic portion of the mystery of Christ: "For in a real sense, Lord Jesus, you are the *plenitudo entium,* the full assemblage of all beings who shelter, and meet, and are for ever united within the mystical bonds of your organism."

This cosmic consecration finds its fulfillment in communion:

An inexhaustible and universal communion is the term of the universal consecration. . . . I pray that this brief and limited contact with the sacramental species may introduce me to a universal and eternal communion with Christ, with his omni-operant will and his boundless mystical Body.[30]

In this and the preceding text Teilhard seems to be using "mystical Body" in a much wider sense than usual, so that it encompasses the full scope of the "cosmic Body." Certainly he is not always scrupulously careful in his use of categories, but the whole thrust of *The Priest* seems to carry him in this direction of affirming the one Body of Christ in its wider scope: "I see your Flesh extend throughout the entire Universe."

FORMA CHRISTI

After the armistice, Teilhard continued to work in Strasbourg, and in the last weeks of December he finished one of his most difficult and concise essays: *Forma Christi.* His preoccupation is the same as always: the full synthesis of his two loves. The catalyst of his work is the same: his anguish at a Christianity which ignores the universe:

> This new essay contains a restatement (since we shall soon be in 1919) of ideas that I have constantly, during the last four years, been trying to express. They relate to the synthesis, in the interior life of the Christian, of love of God and love of the world.
> I am more convinced than ever that our generation understands Christianity in a way that is too *extrinsic* and too *individualistic.* Dogma, both as preached from the pulpit and as it enters into the consciousness of those who receive it: (1) is something up in the air, above the Universe, and with no connection with it; (2) seems to impinge upon only an *insignificant part* of cosmic Reality.[31]

This use of the term "extrinsic" is interesting. It does not mean "extrinsic to the soul" or "extrinsic to the individual person" (the sense devotional books of the time would have given the term), but rather extrinsic to *the universe.* Teilhard has extraordinarily expanded the sphere of man's "intrinsic" realm to include the whole cosmos. For it is Teilhard's experience that man is radically bound up with the universe as such, and so he cannot conceive of an individual redemption and resurrection apart from an eschatological destiny of the entire cosmos:

> The mystical Body of Christ is something more than the totality of souls, because, without there being present in it a specifically material element, souls could not be physically gathered together in Christ. . . . Christ can consummate our unity . . . only if he first encloses us in a material network underlying our *"esse corporeum"* . . . the restoration of the flesh is a phenomenon cosmic rather than individual in order. In virtue of the very essence of materiality, to raise up a single body from death is the same, for God, as to reconstitute a world.
> In fact at no time have there ever been souls wandering in complete

isolation. From the very beginning of time (through a mysterious anticipation or pre-action—a notion we must always bear in mind), and from the first Easter morning in actual reality, "Christ is risen." Since all time, therfore, souls, as they leave this world, have been passing, without any break, into the cosmic train of his Body.[32]

One notes in this passage an amazing anticipation of the work of such men as Boros and Rahner on the "theology of death." It is also clear how central a position the Incarnation and Resurrection occupy in Teilhard's theological cosmology. Because Christ truly assumed a human nature—i.e., became inserted into the *whole* of the material complex of the universe, and because that Body is now glorified, Christ is necessarily invested with a cosmic dimension. Teilhard's model of the cosmic Body is, then, ultimately grounded in his fuller conception of the Incarnation and the Resurrection—a conception that recalls the Greek Fathers and the later Pauline epistles.

NOTE ON THE EVANGELIZATION OF THE NEW AGE

Teilhard begins this essay with a succinct but remarkably penetrating description of modern man's outlook: "The profound religious movement of our age seems to me characterized by the appearance of the universe in human consciousness."[33] Here again Teilhard is speaking at the religious level of insight and experience, but he speaks also as a *modern* religious thinker. He would not deny that the Egyptian and the Greek, the Roman citizen and the medieval monk all had a significant awareness of an *Umwelt,* a contextual cosmos within which the human drama was enacted. But he also believes that he himself represents a new generation that has a particularly fruitful awareness of a dynamic, "organic" universe and man's place in it. He notes sorrowfully that conventional Christianity has not kept pace with this new consciousness of mankind, this altogether legitimate "worldliness," so that "the Christian ideal has ceased to be the shared ideal of humanity." But there is a kind of "secret formula," he argues, which is the key to the whole of creation and will therefore bridge the chasm between Christianity and the rest of humanity: "And this is the formula: *Hoc est corpus meum.*"[34] It is this "universal 'consecration,' universal communion" that will overcome the "schism" between the rest of mankind and Christianity; for what modern man seeks is precisely a Lord "as vast as the Cosmos, as immediate and enveloping as life."

It is in terms of his fundamental model of Christ's cosmic Body, then, that Teilhard will endeavor to speak to the central religious predicament of modern man and resolve it.

THE UNIVERSAL ELEMENT

Teilhard considered this essay, completed early in 1919, as "the most central exposition" of his ideas yet produced.[35] It offers an analysis of the "cosmic consciousness" by which, Teilhard feels, "many men (or all men . . . if they analyzed themselves more carefully) feel the *need* and *capacity* of apprehending a *universal physical* Element in the world."[36] He argues from the force and prevalence of this collective intuition to the real existence of what is perceived:

> If it is to make so constant an appeal to our minds, and to dominate them so powerfully, the Universal Element cannot possibly be an illusion, a *figmentum mentis*. Somewhere there must be a Something that corresponds to cosmic "abstraction" and consciousness.

The familiar argument to the cosmic Body of Christ from the interconnectedness of man (and thus of the incarnate Christ) with the whole universe, recurs here specifically anchored in this collective cosmic consciousness:

> Our perception of the Universal Element does more than *touch on* all our interior experiences, once they are taken far enough and analyzed in sufficient depth: it also has an urge to invade them (or, what comes to the same thing, to emerge from them) in such a way as to force us to take exclusive account of a Unique Essential (*unum necessarium*) in whose activity we are included.

Teilhard goes on explicitly to identify this "Unique Essential" as "the *cosmic Influence* (Life) of Christ."[37]

He is not only arguing that there is a Christic shape to the universe on the ontological level, but he is also insisting that there is in consciousness (on the noetic level of religious intuition or experience) an awareness of this cosmic Element to which faith gives the name of Christ. This position does raise thorny issues, especially regarding naturalistic vs. Christian mysticism, which cannot be explored here. We must, nonetheless, note its importance for Christian spiritual theology. The question has long been debated whether deep experiential intuition of God is a special gift reserved for a few, or whether all Christians have a call to the mystical life.[38] Now, one clear implication of Teilhard's position is a decisive choice of the latter alternative: that all Christians through faith enjoy the capacity to know Christ at a deeper level than the merely notional: viz., the level of religious experience.

One also notes here the Christocentricity of Teilhard's spiritual theology. Whereas some mystics are tempted to conceive of the *unum necessarium* as a contemplation of pure Divinity beyond the particularities of Christ,[39] for Teilhard the *unum necessarium* is precisely the Total Christ, who sums up our every activity and passivity, the whole of humanity, and the whole of the universe.

THE SPIRITUAL POWER OF MATTER

In August of 1919 Teilhard wrote his cousin that he was working on a piece "semi-poetical in style — allegorical in form. The allegory is the story of Elias . . . the whirlwind is matter, which draws with it and liberates those who know how to grasp its spiritual power."[40] That its content represents Teilhard's main concern at the time, we know from his own admission,[41] and it is likewise important in our present context.

As the whirlwind sweeps down upon Elias, he seeks to understand its baffling nature which is somehow "equivocal, turbid, the combined essence of all evil and all goodness."[42] Most baffling of all, this hurricane is not outside, but within Elias' own being, its destiny somehow interwoven with his:

> Always you have, without knowing it, desired me; and always I have been drawing you to me, [the whirlwind is depicted as saying].
> And now I am established on you for life, or for death. . . . He who has once seen me can never forget me: he must either damn himself with me or save me with himself.

As Elias insists on learning the storm's name, it replies: "I am the fire that consumes and the water that overthrows. I am

the love that initiates and the truth that passes away . . .
power, experiment, progress — matter, all this am I."

At issue here is not simply abstract matter or a collection
of objects, but the world conceived precisely as destined to
participate in glory: "You who have grasped that the World —
the World beloved of God — has, even more than individuals,
a soul to be redeemed, open your whole being to my inspiration, and receive the Spirit of the Earth which is to be
saved." Matter is not to be disdained, then, for Christ himself
has blessed and liberated it. Again Teilhard ties this liberation
to the eucharistic consecration understood in its cosmic
scope, and so he suggests again that the universe is but
Christ's Body in its fullest extension:

> "Never say, 'Matter is accursed, Matter is evil'; for there has come
> one who said, 'You will drink poisonous draughts and they shall not
> harm you,' and again, 'Life shall spring forth out of death,' and then
> finally, the words which spell my definitive liberation, 'This is my
> Body.' "[43]

But if the universe is thus liberated as the Body of Christ, it
must function as a vessel of grace for man:

> "Purity does not lie in separation from, but in a deeper penetration
> into the Universe. . . . Oh the beauty of Spirit as it rises up adorned
> with all the riches of the Earth!
> "Son of man, bathe yourself in the ocean of Matter. . . . For it
> cradled you long ago in your preconscious existence; and it is that
> ocean that will raise you up to God."

One might at this point ask in bewilderment what "World,"
what "Universe" Teilhard is discussing. Is it the world simply of rocks and trees, or tenement houses and cadillacs, of
wars and cease-fires? But Teilhard would have us remember
the image of Elias being drawn up *into heaven;* the prophet is
now experiencing everything "on another plane,"[44] so that
"were he to descend again now to the everyday life of
earth . . . he would henceforth be for ever a stranger." This is,
then, the universe in its anticipated eschatological fulfillment — only thus can it claim Elias' total commitment:

> Because Matter, throwing off its veil of restless movement and
> multiplicity, had revealed to him its glorious unity . . . because it had
> for ever withdrawn his heart from all that is merely local or individual,

all that is fragmentary, henceforth for him It alone in its totality would be his father and mother, his family, his race, his unique consuming passion.

Pondering this universe, Elias feels himself confronted not merely by an "It" but by a countenance, a Body, a Person:

> What had been a blind and feral immensity was now becoming expressive and personal; and its former amorphous expanses were now assuming the features of an ineffable face.
>
> A Being was taking form in the totality of space; a Being with the attractive power of a soul, palpable like a body, vast as the sky.

Elias then falls to his knees in the chariot and sings a *Benedictus* in honor of Matter as Christ's Body: "Sap of our souls, Hand of God, Flesh of Christ: it is you, Matter, that I bless."[45] This world, whose "Flesh is so transparent and so agile as to be no longer indistinguishable from spirit," constitutes the divine Milieu itself, for it is from Christ that it draws its form and life. Teilhard, using the Genesis typology, has Elias salute the world as the New Creation, Body of the New Adam: "I acclaim you as the divine Milieu, charged with creative Power, as the Ocean stirred by the Spirit, as the Clay moulded and infused with life by the incarnate Word."

Thus the young Teilhard envisioned and depicted the cosmic Body of Christ. This early vision was nourished and developed throughout his life by his deepening encounter with scripture and the Fathers. Let us now examine that encounter.

CHAPTER THREE

A Sketch of a Theological Heritage

In arguing the case for his "Christian cosmology,"[1] Teilhard often invoked scripture and tradition. He strongly urged his readers to look beyond his own formulations to their verification in writers such as St. Paul, St. John, Irenaeus, Gregory of Nyssa, the Greek Fathers in general, the Russians and Orthodox, Duns Scotus, and Maurice Blondel. Teilhard invoked currents of tradition which he acknowledged knowing only in a passing way through secondary sources,[2] but which he still felt would vindicate his thought. And indeed his friends with biblical and patristic training assured him of the broader foundation of his vision.[3] In this chapter we want to sketch a current of theology in biblical exegesis and tradition which is acknowledged by reputed scholars to be a viable current; and we want to note Teilhard's familiarity with important elements of this current.

TEILHARD AND SCRIPTURE

Whatever be the specialist's final judgment on Teilhard's use of scripture, he himself clearly thought his vision was founded solidly on the revealed texts. As de Lubac observes,

> He reads and continually rereads the Pauline Epistles. He fashions a little notebook for himself that will be his companion for many years in which he copies the Christological texts of the Apostle together with those of St. John. He has pored over tham in a favorable climate during the course of his theological studies; he continues to meditate on them, wishing to understand them "without attenuation and without gloss."[4]

Teilhard characteristically justifies his positions by brief recourse to Pauline and Joannine texts—for example:

> Christ is quite simply Omega. To demonstrate this fundamental propo-

sition I need only refer to a long series of Johannine and especially
Pauline texts where the physical supremacy of Christ over the Universe is proclaimed in magnificent terms.[5]

Scriptural citations abound in Teilhard's writings, although
the specific texts referred to number only about fifteen. The
texts are not merely decorative, however, nor even corro-
borative; they are more like points of departure for the
elaboration of Teilhard's notion of the cosmic Christ.[6] Such
neologisms as *pléromisation* and *cephalisation* are clearly
Pauline in inspiration, and Teilhard's many laudatory references to Paul and John leave little doubt of his devotion to
them.

Teilhard numbered among his lifelong friends the highly
respected Pauline exegete Joseph Huby, S.J., who was a
fellow-scholastic at Hastings and continued later on to coun-
sel him. Gabriel M. Allegra, O.F.M., the President of the
Franciscan Biblical Institute of Peking and Hong Kong, be-
friended him over a three-year period during which they discussed key Pauline texts at great length.[7]

Thus Teilhard, though not himself an exegete, sought to
root his vision in scripture through his own study and through
the help of scholarly friends. Let us now examine some key
themes as delineated by exegetes, which seem to provide
solid ground for his theology of the universe.

The Biblical Concept of Body

The category of "body" is one of the richest, theologically,
in the Bible.[8] The apparently simple affirmation that Christ
has a human body is therefore pregnant with deep theological
implications that might easily escape a modern reader. Robinson points out, e.g., that the Hebrew notion of "body" con-
noted union with, rather than distinction from, the rest of
nature; and he goes on to show the close link between this
Hebraic tradition and Pauline thought: ". . . man as "flesh" is
related to God in this way, not as an individual, but as part of
the whole world order. Here again the typical Old Testament
presuppositions come to the surface in Pauline thought."[9]

It follows, in this perspective, that Jesus as man, through
his flesh, is entwined "in the bundle of life with all men and

nature." But what of the glorified Christ? Durrwell, insisting
that Paul's Captivity Letters speak of the incarnate and risen
Christ rather than the pre-existing Word, goes on to maintain
that precisely in that incarnate, risen Christ, the world "pulls
itself together . . . and becomes a cosmos, an ordered universe."[10] For Huby, too, the world is "based on [Christ] as
upon its focal point, where all the threads, all the generating
lines of the universe are knotted together and coordinated."[11]
Faricy stresses the organic character of Paul's cosmic soteriology in which the cosmos appears as engrafted in the
glorious body-person of Christ.[12]

Redemption of the Universe

Jesus, then, by virtue of his Body both in its earthly and
(especially) in its glorified state, has the most intimate rapport
with the universe. This rapport finds expression in the scriptural teachings that Christ's redemptive activity extends even
to the universe. Lyonnet points out that this conception is
deeply rooted in the Old Testament, for which "the history of
salvation did not begin only with Abraham or Noah, nor even
with Adam . . . [but] with creation itself."[13] What had been
more or less vague "suggestions" became in Paul's teaching a
"clearly defined doctrine." Although the redemption of the
universe is only a consequence of man's redemption, Lyonnet
insists strongly on its reality: "The universe will not be content merely to look on from the outside at this triumph of
redeemed humanity. . . . The material universe is called to
share in the future of the children of God."[14] "The benefits of
the redemption," echoes Huby, "thus extend in a certain
measure to all."[15]

It is of more than passing interest that this section of
Romans 8, with its vindication of the cosmic dimensions of
Christ's saving action, is one of Teilhard's favorite biblical
passages. Indeed, Lyonnet concludes his technical exegesis
with these observations heavily redolent of Teilhard:

> From the fact that the redemption of the body extends to the whole
> universe, it follows that the work of man—his efforts to master the
> material universe, to draw out its secrets, to domesticate and utilize it,
> to transform brute matter into instruments of greater and greater

perfection . . . all such human work acquires a value for eternity. . . .
For us Christians every new advance in the harnessing of nature by
man, every new conquest of itself enters into the divine plan. It
continues creation. . . . Such advances prepare in a certain, though
enigmatic way for the future redemption of the universe.[16]

Colossians 1:15-20

This key Pauline text, one of Teilhard's favorites, was
discussed at length by Allegra and Teilhard. Allegra commu-
nicated to Teilhard the Scotist exegesis which has become a
cornerstone of Franciscan theology: precisely as God-man,
Christ is the first willed of all creatures, and all else has been
created through, in, and for him. "I do not hesitate to say that
St. Paul really gives us the cosmic dimensions of Christ,"
Allegra concludes, ". . . and not merely those Mediterranean
dimensions that many Christians attribute to him."[17]

Because God wanted "all things to be reconciled through
Christ and for Christ,"[18] the "pleroma" or fullness of the
entire creation is said to dwell in Christ. And because of this
"pleroma" theme the famous hymn of Col. 1:15-20 becomes
a main source for the exegetical study of Christ's cosmic
dimension.[19] How is "pleroma" to be understood? Most
scholars today reject St. Thomas' interpretation of "fullness
of graces," just as they reject St. John Chrysostom's reading
"plenitude of divinity."[20]

But we should not simply imagine Christ's fullness shining
out to a distant world as the sun shines upon the earth.
Rather, as Durrwell explains, "pleroma" means that all things
are filled with Christ and abide in Christ.[21] Mooney links the
notion to Christ's redemptive action conceived in its wider
scope and stresses the inclusion of the entire cosmos in
Christ.[22]

In this same hymn (Col. 1:15-20) Christ's headship is spoken of (v. 18), and the exegetical notes of the *Jerusalem Bible*
point out that this headship extends to the cosmos itself.
Specifically in reference to the verse affirming that God wished all perfection to be found in Christ, the *Jerusalem Bible*
again stresses Christ's cosmic headship: ". . . the incarnation
and resurrection make Christ head not only of the entire
human race, but of the entire created cosmos, so that every-

thing that was involved in the fall is equally involved in the salvation."

Ephesians 1:9-10; 2:10

This equally significant text, also discussed at length by Allegra and Teilhard,[23] raises even more directly the issue of Christ as head of the cosmos: "It was God's loving design to bring everything together under Christ, as head, everything in heaven and everything on earth."[24] Exegetes point out, first of all, that it is clearly a question of *all* things. Lyonnet writes:

> The epistle to the Ephesians describes explicitly the salvific plan of God as the recapitulation of all things in Christ—not just all men but all things; so much so that nothing that exists should escape the vital influence of Christ.[25]

The verb used here, $'\alpha\nu\alpha\kappa\epsilon\phi\alpha\lambda\alpha\iota\omega\mu\alpha\iota$, has as its root meaning "to head up," so that Christ is affirmed to be reuniting "the whole body of creation" into "an organism with himself as head."[26] In Eph. 2:10, moreover, Christ is declared to be "the head of every Sovereignty and Power"; many exegetes see here the clear affirmation that Christ is head of the entire universe.[27]

At this point a very interesting question arises: If Christ is head of the cosmos as he is head of the Church, and if the Church is his Body, is it not also the case that the cosmos must also be conceived as his Body? Put quite simply, "head" suggests "body." For Pauline thought itself, then, is not the cosmos the Body of Christ? Of course we do not have an explicit text affirming this—nor do we have one denying it. Mooney nonetheless observes that Paul reserves the term "Body" for redeemed humanity,[28] and Best draws a subtle distinction that ends up restricting "Body" to the Church:

> The headship of Christ is conceived in at least two ways, as over the Church, and as over all creation . . . but the headship over all creation is an overlordship; the headship over Christians . . . is also a headship of source. Christians as the Body are united to the Head and draw their life therefrom.[29]

Schnackenburg is content to call the question "disputed,"[30] Faricy insists that Paul does conceive of the universe as

Christ's cosmic Body,[31] and such exegetes as Dibelius and Schlier call this latter position "very likely."[32]

Comparing the Pauline conception with parallel notions in Greek and Roman culture, Schlier notes that Paul does (at least occasionally, as in Col. 2:19 and Eph. 4:16) use the term "body" in the sense of "cosmos."[33]

Conclusion

The foregoing discussion has perhaps provided some indication of how many exegetes feel Pauline thought expresses Christ's intimate relationship with the cosmos. As the reader is doubtless well aware, there are innumerable other themes which would require detailed study before a complete picture of that relationship could be sketched out. Both the Pauline and the Joannine visions encompass many diverse emphases, of which Teilhard's is only one – and a selective one at that. As Rideau observes, Teilhard's citations of St. Paul are taken mainly from "humanist" or "cosmic" passages, rather than passages like Romans 1 with its dialectic of human sin and divine wrath.[34]

Not only is Teilhard's use of Paul selective, but it also involves transposing Paul into a different key, as it were, by emphasizing the cosmological rather than the strictly soteriological dimensions of his gospel. Mooney expresses this point well:

> The source of the whole difficulty here is . . . that Paul's message is a message of salvation. He interests himself in the world of nature and man's relationships to that world only in so far as these have religious meaning. He has no intention whatsoever of explaining *how* Christ is Lord of the cosmos. For Teilhard, on the other hand, a cosmology is at the heart of his whole system, and his appeals to St. Paul are made with the precise purpose of explaining this "how" and of using the Apostle's thought as a point of departure for his own vision of the world.[35]

But even given all these qualifications, should not Teilhard's use of Paul to stress the intimate relationship of Christ to the cosmos be judged fundamentally legitimate? As Mooney goes on to point out, the restoration of the whole universe in Christ does constitute a "dominant theme" of the Captivity Epistles. The specialists are admittedly not unani-

mous on the point; and, at any rate, a final judgment of
Teilhard's use of Paul can come only after an exhaustive
study of both men's thought. But all the major expositors of
Teilhard go out of their way to vindicate his use of Paul,[36]
and we feel that the brief exposition just completed indicates
sufficiently for present purposes the strong logic of such a
vindication: If Christ is Head of the redeemed cosmos, that
cosmos is indeed his Body.

TEILHARD AND THE FATHERS

In his earliest essay of the war period, Teilhard was already claiming the authority of the Fathers as well as scripture, to defend his concept of Christ's Body:

> The Body of Christ is not, as some unenterprising thinkers would have
> us believe, the extrinsic or juridical association of men. . . . It must be
> understood rather in that full sense which St. John and St. Paul and
> the Fathers affirmed and loved.[37]

Teilhard continued, in later writings, to invoke the Fathers
both in a general way and with references to specific Fathers,[38] and his proponents are in accord in acknowledging
the patristic antecedents of his thought. Not that he was a
patristic scholar,[39] but he did believe that his work was solidly grounded in the Fathers, and still more important, he was
unequivocally encouraged in his conviction by such theologians as de Lubac, d'Ales, and de Solages, who were themselves very deeply read in the Fathers.

Even if it were only through this indirect relation to the
Fathers through his friends, Teilhard clearly has the right to
trace his "spiritual ancestry" to the Fathers. As with scripture in the preceding pages, so here we intend to furnish only
the briefest sort of sketch in this area of patristic support. It
should be noted, though, that Emile Mersch's magisterial
work on the mystical Body of Christ, which is our own major
source, contains "a thorough summary of both the Greek and
Latin traditions" in the issue of the cosmic Christ.[40] This
important work was, moreover, published in 1933, more than
twenty years before Teilhard's death; so it clearly indicates
the level of scholarship reached and readily available during
Teilhard's life. Add to this the fact that Mersch studied at

Louvain under P. Charles, S.J., and J. Maréchal, S.J., both good friends of Teilhard who corresponded with him and counselled him, and it is hard to imagine that Teilhard would be oblivious of Mersch's work.[41]

Melito of Sardis

Melito, Bishop of Sardis, was a rather prolific writer of the Asia Minor school in the second century. He does not deal directly with the Body of Christ theme, but he does stress God's dominion over all creation in an extraordinarily suggestive way. One text in particular is highly significant for our purposes. In treating of God's powerful immanence, Melito makes explicit use of the "body" figure:

> Understand how within you is what is called the soul: by it the eye sees, by it the ear hears, by it the mouth speaks: and how it employs the whole body. And whensoever He pleases to remove the soul from the body, it falls and goes to decay. From this . . . understand how God also moves the whole world by his power, like the body, and that whensoever it pleases him to withdraw his power, the whole world, also, like the body, will fall and go to decay.[42]

The world is like a body, and just as the soul activates and unifies man's body, so God activates and unifies the world. One cannot help reflecting how warmly Teilhard would respond to this second-century text.

Irenaeus

St. Irenaeus, the most significant Christian theologian of the second century,[43] is referred to by Teilhard, who also discussed him with his scholarly friends.[44] As Teilhard himself observes, "One finds an astonishing anticipation — based it is true, rather on a mystical viewpoint than on empirical fact — of our modern views of progress in the Greek Fathers — Irenaeus, for example."[45] Whatever be thought of Teilhard's exegesis, certainly Irenaeus' concept of "recapitulation" of all things in Christ provides a rich wellspring for cosmic theology. The dependence on Eph. 1:10 is obvious and common knowledge; but Irenaeus does more than simply echo the category — as Maloney puts it, he "advances the content of the term."[46] He uses it so often and in such a variety of contexts, in fact, that many scholars argue that it provides the key to his whole soteriology.[47]

For Irenaeus, it is the whole history of salvation that is summed up or "recapitulated" in Christ.[48] But it is also the cosmos itself: "Christ has therefore in his work of recapitulation summed up all things, waging war against our enemy and indeed crushing him who had led us away captive in Adam."[49] Through the Church the entire universe enters into the "new creation" spoken of by St. Paul. "God's created world is not intrinsically evil, according to Irenaeus, but it must be 'absorbed by' the immortality and incorruptibility of Christ."[50]

Man and universe are thus absorbed into Christ, not definitively all at once, but in the context of a growing development destined for completion only in the eschaton:

> Man's growth as well as that of the cosmos is a process of constant maturity into the greater fullness of being. This fullness will not be reached in this life but in the life to come. The present world will not be destroyed or annihilated but only transfigured into a new manner of existence.[51]

We shall see later how important this notion of growing cosmic transformation is for Teilhard, and we shall also note the central place eschatological fulfillment has in his system.

Origen

Origen has been called "the most outstanding theologian of pre-Nicene times, if not of the whole Patristic period."[52] Maloney has drawn attention to his influence on Gregory of Nyssa, Evagrius of Pontus, and pseudo-Dionysius, through whom his speculations spread to such Western writers as St. Bernard, Meister Eckhart, and St. John of the Cross.[53] Our necessarily restricted scope enables us to cite only a few of his many ideas of significance for a cosmic vision of Christ's Body.

Like Melito, Origen sees the universe as a single organism "informed," as it were, by God himself:

> Although the whole world is arranged in diverse parts and functions, we must not suppose that its condition is one of discord and self-contradiction; but as our one body is composed of many members

and is held together by one soul, so we should, I think, accept the opinion that the universe is, as it were, an immense organism, held together by the power and reason of God as by one soul.[54]

Note Origen's use of Paul's image (1 Cor. 12) to explain Christ's Body, and especially the cosmic import he gives to that image. Another significant theme is that of the risen Christ's omnipresence:

> I think that the saints as they depart from this life will remain in some place situated on the earth, which the divine Scripture calls "paradise" . . . Christ however is everywhere and his presence extends into all things; nor are we any longer to think of him as being confined within those narrow limits of his earthly, unglorified body which he once lived in for our sakes, so that it was then possible to think of him as being enclosed in some one place.[55]

Elsewhere, Origen considers explicitly the possibility that the Body of the omnipresent, glorified Christ comprises "the whole universality of creation."[56]

Athanasius

In the great fourth-century Doctor of the Church, Athanasius, it is not simply "God" who is said to dominate the gigantic "body" of the world, but specifically the divine *Word*. And this domination is placed in strict parallel with the domination of Christ's humanity by that same Word:

> The Greek philosophers say that the world is a great body. And in this they are right. For we see that the world and its parts are sensible things. If, then, the Word of God resides in this world which is a body; if he is present in each and every thing, is there anything strange or absurd in our claim that the Word is present in a man? [57]

Mersch insists that this text envisages the mystical Body as representing "not human nature only, but the entire universe," and he capitalizes on the fact that the notion is extremely prevalent both in Irenaeus and throughout patristic thought.[58]

A well known objection to the concept of the cosmic Christ being set forth in this essay, is that such a concept would jeopardize the distinction between nature (creation) and grace (redemption). From Athanasius and the other Fathers, however, we learn that both these orders are somehow encompassed in the single deifying action of the Word through the Spirit:

> It is in the Spirit that the Logos glorifies creation and deifies it and adopts and conducts it to the Father. . . . The Spirit does not make part of created things, but is proper to the divinity of the Father and it is in him that the Logos deifies the creatures.[59]

Grace is seen as not so much a "thing" or even an "accident" in the Aristotelian sense, but rather as the force of God's saving presence, extending to the entire universe.

Gregory of Nyssa

The great fourth-century Cappadocian Father Gregory of Nyssa is one of Teilhard's explicitly credited sources,[60] and it is not difficult to see a real parallel in their conceptions of the Christian economy. Gregory, like Teilhard, stressed the dynamic, majestic unity of the divine plan extending from its conception, through creation, to the very Parousia. In a significant passage which is cited and discussed by Mersch, Gregory explicitly affirms that the whole of creation is brought into Christ's Body:

> Since he is in all, he takes into himself all who are united with him by the participation of his body; he makes them all members of his body, in such wise that the many members are but one body. Having thus united us with himself and himself with us, and having become one with us in all things, he makes his own all that is ours. But the greatest of all our goods is submission to God, which brings all creation into harmony. Then . . . all creation becomes one body, all are grafted one upon the other, and Christ speaks of the submission of his body to the Father as his own submission.[61]

Cyril of Alexandria

The fifth-century Alexandrian theologian Cyril contributes to the golden age of Christology by stressing in a particular way Christ's immanence. He conceives of this immanence, not as a passive, inert omnipresence, but rather as a transforming force that divinizes man and through man "effects also a degree of incorruptibility in the non-human cosmos."[62]

Cyril describes in the strongest of terms the union of Christ with the members of his Body:

In his Wisdom and in accordance with the counsels of the Father, Christ has found a means of bringing and welding us into unity with God and with one another, although by reason of our souls and bodies we are each distinct personalities.

Through one body, which is his own, he blesses, by a mysterious communion, those who believe, and he makes them concorporal with himself and with one another.

Who can now separate them or deprive them of their physical union? They have been bound together into union with Christ by means of his one holy body.[63]

This text is particularly interesting to students of Teilhard because, as we shall note below, Teilhard stresses precisely this *physical* union of Christ with his cosmic Body. Mersch suggests that the same concern lest that union be interpreted in some merely juridical or moral sense, induced Cyril to stress Christ's physical union with his members:

The heretics maintain . . . that the union of the Son and the Father is like that which exists among ourselves; to wit, a union of resemblance and agreement of wills; in short, a moral union. But, continues the Saint, bringing in the doctrine of the Mystical Body, is it true that we are bound together only by a moral union? Does not the sacred text itself tell us something more, of a real "physical" union?[64]

Conclusion

In the foregoing, necessarily cursory and selective survey, we could not refer the reader to the many other Fathers whose work is relevant: St. Ephraem, St. Gregory Nazianzen, St. Maximus — and, in the West, Tertullian, Ambrose, Augustine, and others. No mention could be made, either, of some pertinent liturgical texts in both East and West. Still, the patristic indications which have been furnished should at least suggest the wider context in which Teilhard's concept of the Christic character of the universe, of the cosmic Body, must be judged. Far from innovating irresponsibly, Teilhard was "in a new context conditioned by new scientific advances, forging a more exact bond with an ancient tradition running through so many long centuries."[65]

TEILHARD AND THE THEOLOGIANS

It has already been noted above, that in the scholastic period the concept of Christ's Body suffers a real decline and a certain "juridicism" gains ascendancy.[66] Most scholastics either deny outright that material things can pertain to Christ's Body, or they do not even raise the question.[67] It would be a mistake, however, to draw too simplistic a picture of a long and complex theological period. Careful research does reveal some positive, if isolated, contributions to a more cosmic concept of the Body of Christ.

Thomas Aquinas

Despite some compatibility problems between Aquinas and Teilhard, theologians do point out several areas of convergence.[68] We would note here particularly Thomas' concept of the eternal destiny of the universe:

> Because all corporeal beings exist in some way for man, it is fitting that after the last judgment the state of the entire corporeal universe will be transformed, so that it will be in harmony with what will then be the state of man. And since men will then be incorruptible, the present state of corruptibility will be removed from the corporeal universe . . . and since men will not only be freed from corruption, but clothed in glory, the material universe must also acquire in its way a certain splendor of glory.[69]

If this text is considered in the light of the Pauline concept of glory, which (as noted above) implies a very special participation in the glorified Christ, then we have here a significant, if implicit, reaffirmation of the Christic destiny of the whole cosmos.

John Duns Scotus

Teilhard draws explicitly on the Scotist notion of the Incarnation,[70] and Allegra has recorded his excited reaction to one Scotist treatment of the subject: "It is a marvelous page! What a plain but unique power of expression. Behold cosmic theology, the theology of the future!" At a later point in their discussion, Teilhard is quoted as affirming, "I see now that Scotus is truly a powerful thinker and that his texts manifest a genuine Pauline *parresia*."[71]

Certainly the Teilhard-Allegra encounter is one of the more interesting chapters in Teilhard's rather curtailed life of dialogue; and it is clear from Allegra's careful reconstruction of their discussions that key Scotist concepts significantly buttress Teilhard's cosmic Christology:

> Had [Adam's] fall been the cause of the predestination of Christ, then the supreme work of God would have been merely incidental. Now, it seems most unreasonable to maintain that God would have foregone such a masterpiece simply because of a [hypothetical] good deed of Adam, such as it would have been if Adam had not sinned. The glory of all creatures can indeed never be as intensively great as the glory of Christ. . . . Thus the Christ-man, as well as all the elect, was foreseen and predestined to grace and glory even prior to foreseeing his passion as a remedy against the fall, just as a physician has a greater interest in the health of a patient than in prescribing medicine for him.[72]

What is affirmed in this profound theological vision is not that Christ is simply first in a series: number one on a spectrum of many juxtaposed intentions on the same plane. Rather, Christ is depicted as the key, the principle, the exemplar and final cause for all the rest of creation. Unger not only summarizes all this quite eloquently, but he links the affirmations directly to the Pauline texts so central for Teilhard:

> By the universal and absolute primacy of Christ we mean that Christ was predestined by God absolutely and primarily for his own glory, then as the universal Scope of all creation, and as universal Exemplar of all creatures . . . in the order of nature and of grace and of glory from the very beginning . . . all the inanimate creation is united in and through him. . . . Thus Christ holds the first place in all things (Col. 1:18) and in him are all things summarized and brought to a head (Eph. 1:10).[73]

Thus the cosmos itself has a Christic shape, for Christ's human nature becomes "the *motif* the Divine Architect was to carry out in the rest of creation. In Christ's soul God saw mirrored the choirs of angels; after his body the visible world was sculptured. The whole universe is full of Christ."[74] The cosmos has not only a Christic shape, but also—as we have noted—a Christic fulfillment.

What is really at issue, Wildiers points out in what might seem an excessively abstruse discussion of the order of divine intentions, is the very concrete issue of Christ's relationship to the cosmos. Is it merely accidental and juridical (as the

Thomist position might imply), or is it rather intrinsic and indeed *organic?* Wildiers' conclusion is worth citing in full:

> . . . this interpretation ascribes to Christ a central function in the cosmos—a function, that is, not to be understood in purely moral or juridical terms. In the beginning it was oriented upon him, so that we are indeed right to say that he is the beginning and the end, the Alpha and Omega, of all things. Christ's place in the cosmos is an organic function: that is, the world is centered on Christ in respect of its intrinsic structure, in its actual mode of being. . . .[75]

The significance of the Scotist position for a radically Christic cosmology is evident, as is Teilhard's close affinity with that venerable position.

Peter Galatinus

In his apologetical work on the mysteries of the Catholic "Truth," Galatinus explicitly inserts all creation in the fullness of the mystical Body by virtue of Christ's mission to restore all things.[76] This influential Franciscan theologian confronted the rabbinical tradition according to which the Father's foreknowledge of original sin causes him to ponder anew whether to create. As Mersch succinctly summarizes Galatinus' position, the economy of creation-salvation is seen as recast by the Father in a Christic mold:

> But the Son intervened, promising to become man in order to restore all. Then, in view of the Incarnation, God created all things. Therefore, since they were created for the sake of Christ, all things belong to the Mystical Body by the very fact of their existence.[77]

Ambrogio Catarino Polito

The brilliant and daring sixteenth-century theologian Catarino, "one of the most active influences at the Council of Trent,"[78] explicitly insists that the entire universe is included in the mystical Body, arguing from his theory, much influenced by Scotus,[79] of Christ's predestation. Again we owe this succinct summary to Mersch:

> So excellent is the predestation of Christ . . . that it includes God's whole plan with regard to the universe. God willed his incarnate Son before all things; hence he created and ordained all things for him, so that Christ and the recapitulation of all things of all things in Christ constitute the sole purpose and the sole *raison d'être* of the order of nature as well as of the order of grace.[80]

Cardinal de Bérulle

The recent revival of interest in the great seventeenth-century French Cardinal is due largely to the work of one of Teilhard's teachers, Henri Bremond, who "brought to life again, with a magical art, [his] most beautiful pages."[81] Allegra touched upon Bérulle's work in his conversations with Teilhard,[82] and de Lubac affirms that Teilhard "might have read, and perhaps did" Bérulle's *Discours de l'état et des grandeurs de Jésus.*[83]

Bérulle's dependence on Paul is clear, and Bellemare argues that the fundamental inspiration of the Cardinal's whole theology is the Pauline concept of life "in Christ."[84] Moreover, Bérulle's acquaintance with the Fathers is impressive; Mersch stresses particularly the influence of the Greek Fathers upon Bérulle's concept of the efficacy of the Incarnation.[85]

The influence of Duns Scotus is also quite apparent in Bérulle. He holds, for instance, that the creature's relation to the Creator is not accidental but essential,[86] and — more important for present purposes — that the Incarnation ought not be conceived as contingent upon the Fall or as distinct from the divine Will itself.[87] Indeed, in many other areas of his theology Bérulle so closely "allies himself with Scotus"[88] that it becomes difficult to separate the subtle interweaving of Scotist elements into the whole fabric of his thought.

Bérulle's spiritual theology is grounded in his concept of creation; he argues that in and through creation God gives creatures their "own" existence, but by the same act they are decisively ordered, in virtue of their created existence, back to God.[89] Bellemare notes a dynamic quality in Bérulle's vision:

> His originality begins to appear when he ties to the relational character of creation a dynamic aspect. He often describes a movement toward God, an instinct of return to him, impressed upon existence by the Creator.[90]

But this theocentric character of his theology is given a markedly Christic thrust in the writings of the mature Bérulle. The Cardinal is said to have undergone a kind of "conversion" at the age of thirty two, which carried him beyond his more abstract speculation to a specifically Christic orientation.[91] And this conversion, which Bérulle himself refers to as a "Copernican revolution,"[92] owes much to the Greek Fathers and the Scotist tradition.[93]

The later Bérulle thus grounded his theological interpretation of creation in a sort of Pauline cosmic Christology. "*Omnia per ipsum facta sunt,*" he writes, "because he is the exemplar of creation."[94] And he addresses Christ as *conditor* and milieu of creation:

> O humanity divinely subsisting, divinely living, divinely operating! You are worthy, in this divine and infinite quality which you possess, indeed infinitely worthy, to rule all that is created and all that is able to be created. . . . Even insensible nature is sensible to your commands, as we see with the tempests, with the winds and thunder and restless waves which obey you, *majestate conditoris.* . . . You are the milieu of created and uncreated being.[95]

Bérulle frequently refers to the Incarnation as God's "work of works, his mystery of mysteries."[96] Like the Fathers, he understands the Incarnation as not simply the assumption by the Word of an isolated human nature, but as somehow the transformation of the whole of creation: "O grandeur of the mystery of the Incarnation, to establish within created being an infinite state and dignity."[97] He sees the Incarnation as "the singular means which divine Wisdom has found to join earth with heaven as at a point and center," so that the Savior of man becomes the "Redeemer of the universe."[98] As center of heaven and earth, drawing all being into coherence, "Christ sums up the world and God."[99]

At his "third birth" (resurrection), Jesus is described by Bérulle as receiving from his Father a body "far more glorious than the sun [that] contains within its immense grandeur both earth and sun, all the stars and all the expanse of the heavens, a body that rules all bodies and all heavenly spirits."[100]

Maurice Blondel

Although space limitations force us to omit consideration of such relevant theologians and spiritual writers as Francis de Sales, Cardinal Newman, and Cardinal Pie, we cannot conclude our investigation without some discussion of one thinker who, at least in this area, towers above them all: Maurice Blondel.

Blondel's direct influence on Teilhard is well known.[101] The substantial link between the two thinkers was Fr. Auguste Valensin, S.J., who kept Teilhard informed of Blondel's writings until the first two exchanged letters in 1919. It was not long after that they met personally and found themselves "in agreement on essentials."[102] Teilhard observes that "certain parts of [Blondel's] thought have had considerable effect on me," particularly "the meaning of action . . . and the notion of 'pan-Christism.' "[103] Except for the oral conversations included in Allegra's book, Teilhard cites Blondel explicitly only once, in *Comment je crois,* but he acknowledges his influence implicitly elsewhere,[104] and there is no doubt that the minds of the two great thinkers "were in many ways akin."[105]

The impact of St. Paul upon Blondel's theology is significant.[106] Like Teilhard, Blondel manifests a decidedly mystical thrust which is Christic in character. He gives great prominence to the cosmic Christ, in whom all things hold together—the Christ who is the head of all creation[107]—and he himself notes that his concept of Christ's "universal function" was refined "above all through reading the mystics (the great realists among men)."[108] It is particularly interesting to see Blondel opt for the Scotist rather than the Thomist current of theology, for such a commitment was by no means easy in the late nineteenth century, when the highest authorities of the Church were bending every effort to promote the Angelic Doctor.[109] In the intolerant and bigoted atmosphere of that time, Blondel must have felt (like Teilhard somewhat later) that he was swimming very much against the current. All this makes it the more extraordinary that Blondel could confront theologians with a seminal cosmic Christology as a creative alternative to their view of Christ:

> If in the study of sensible reality and even of the lowest forms of existence we find, in so far as we try to disengage some objective element, that our thought loses itself in an endless flight and contin-

ually goes beyond itself . . . it is perhaps because we can never touch being at any point without encountering at least implicitly the source and bond of all being, the universal Realizer. Neither sensation, nor science, nor philosophy terminate absolutely in themselves. . . . There are two theological opinions, either of which we are at present free to choose: according to one, the Incarnation of the Word has as its motive simply original sin in view of the Redemption upon the Cross; according to the other, the original plan of creation embraces the mystery of the Man-God in such sort that the fall of man determined only the sorrowful and humiliating conditions which Christ accepted together with the superabundance of grace and dignity which is the fruit of this superabundance of love. It is possible that the Church will decide between these one day, and in favour of the second.[110]

For Blondel as for Scotus, the natural order is not complete in itself; rather it is open to and finds its center and completion in a higher focus, the cosmic Christ. This openness was captured by Blondel in a remarkable image which Lacroix succinctly paraphrases:

Blondel once summed up his philosophy in a striking comparison. . . . In the Pantheon of Agrippa, at Rome, the immense dome has no keystone. Instead there is a central opening through which comes all the light that enters the building. So does the edifice of our soul reach up.[111]

The Pantheon can culminate in its aperture of light, of course, because it is well conceived as an organic whole, and Blondel's point is that the same is true of the cosmos:

The generally held notion, even the scientific notion of the body . . . is extremely deficient—the action of our presence is virtually boundless; we act *in toto* as we undergo, direct and make specific within ourselves the action of the Whole. Therefore there is not simply a universal interdependence . . . but an interpenetration; we are literally made up of one another.[112]

Man forms with the cosmos one evolutionary totality, one living being, as it were. This ordered whole has an evolutionary thrust, is hierarchically structured, and abides in the divine milieu:

The great hidden truth in evolutionism is this—that the subject is shaped out of its very object, *de limo terrae,* that the world does indeed form a system, like a single animal, that there is not just an ideal plan and a logical sequence, but an ascending kinship and filiation as well, the same food, the same blood, nature feeding on and rising out of nature, while God is still continually in everything, everywhere, for everything.[113]

But if God is present in all things which form one organic totality, what is the bond which unites this whole? Blondel felt that the "substantial bond" which Leibniz, e.g., had sought, is none other than "the universal Mediator, the Word Incarnate."[114]

The cosmic perspective thrust upon mankind by the sciences challenges the Christian's commitment to Christ. What does the "prisoner of the tabernacle," the "Jesus meek and mild" of popular piety, have to do with the cosmic expanse of millions of light-years and the microscopic realm of subatomic particles? This was a real problem for Blondel. In a paragraph that anticipates Teilhard, he affirms:

> Our world has expanded through the social and natural sciences. One cannot remain true to Catholicism and be content with a mediocre explanation, a limited outlook which represents Christ as an accident of history, isolating Him in the Cosmos as if He were an episode without proper time and place. One cannot represent Him as an intruder, an alien in the crushing and hostile immensity of the universe. Well before the "Loisyism" of the little red books I was clearly and profoundly aware of the options at hand: either to fall back into a murderous symbolism, or go forward towards a realism which is self-consistent throughout, towards a total reality which puts the metaphysics of Christianity in accord with the mystical theology lived by the saints and even by the faithful following. Having always been a *maximist* I was deeply gratified to see the efforts of the minimists rebuffed. The parting of the ways has been reached, and we are led to the *instauratio tota in Christo: de Christo numquam satis*.[115]

Blondel sees two significant implications of his choice for Scotism over Thomism: (1) things are ultimately intelligible only in Christ; and (2) Christ is the final cause of all creation. His development of these points is both eloquent and philosophically technical.[116] He even uses the term "pan-Christism" to emphasize his teaching that all things find their explanation in Christ: "I aspire to a doctrine of being, of life, of personality, seeking the ultimate explanation from the heights to the depths, and finding it not in a panlogism, but in a pan-Christism."[117]

He ties this pan-Christism to a cosmic view of the Incarnation conceived after the manner of the Greek Fathers, as not merely the union of the Word with one individual nature but as the point of contact and divinization of the natural order with the supernatural:

> It is always the mystery of the *Verbum caro factum* and the *caro Verbum facta*. The one is only possible through the other. The world is unquestionably divinized. . . . We breathe the air He breathed, and something of Him is circulating within us.[118]

Just as the Pauline vision is characterized by an extraordinary Christic unity, so Blondel feels that his "pan-Christism" provides the unifying theme of the divine economy, drawing the various moments into cohesion:

> . . . it is necessary that Christ be all that I have affirmed in order that the authentic teaching of the Church be expressly that which it is. And one thus comprehends more and more deeply the unity of the divine Plan in creation, in the Incarnation, in supernaturalization.[119]

"Pan-Christism" is, then, far from marginal to Blondel's system. In fact scholars argue that in its various forms it constitutes one of Blondel's key ideas.[120] In another move that anticipates Teilhard, Blondel himself explicitly ties his theme of Christ as substantial bond to the eucharistic action which lifts all the elements to a higher, Christic level. In a letter to Teilhard, he observes that

> the question raised by Leibnitz and des Bosses concerning transubstantiation during the Eucharist leads us to conceive of Christ, without detriment to the constituent monads, as the bond which makes substantiation possible, the vivifying agent for all of creation: *vinculum perfectionis*.[121]

He sees the eucharistic transubstantiation, moreover, as a prelude and anticipation of the final transformation of all things into Christ:

> Transubstantiation, by substituting for the natural being of the bread and wine the *Vinculum ipsius Christi*, appears to us as preluding, under the veils of mystery, the final assimilation, the supreme incorporation of everything that is into the incarnate Word. . . .[122]

In Blondel, then, we have a remarkable cosmic vision which anticipates Teilhard's "Mass on the World": everything which exists is somehow, by anticipation, assimilated in the eucharistic Body of Christ, exemplar, vehicle, and realization of the substantial Bond of the universe.

Mersch

Throughout this survey we have used as a point of reference Emile Mersch's work on the mystical Body—a work which has made a major contribution to recent cosmic Christology. It is predominantly positive (historical) theology, however, so that the author seldom proffers speculations of his own. His views do emerge, however, and quite clearly, as in this comment on the scholastic period:

> Augustine had given an interpretation which greatly minimized [Romans 8:19-20]. Through fear of Manichaeism and Origenism he declared that "all creation" refers in reality only to man. . . . For a time Augustine's authority prevailed in the exegesis of the passage, but finally the evidence carried the day. Forced, so to speak, By Scripture itself, the Scholastics at last find the courage to paint the grandiose but vague vision of a universe breathless with expectancy and straining after the divine adoption. To account for this restlessness of material things they have recourse to the union that exists between man and the world. . . . But the world does not have to wait until the Last Judgment, in order to be included in the economy of salvation. . . . We have quoted Suarez' words: "He is Lord of all things." This universal dominion is unanimously admitted by the Scholastics, although all do not understand it in exactly the same sense. Christ as man is Lord of all, because all things enter into his work of redemption.
>
>   The same formula may also serve as our conclusion. By reason of their continuity with man, material things receive a certain prolongation of the influx of grace, while at the same time they serve in their way to transmit that influx. Christ, therefore, is their Head, inasmuch as they fulfill this role in the economy of redemption. The whole Christ is the Saviour, together with the whole of humanity; but the whole of humanity is man, together with the entire universe. Therefore the whole Christ is Christ together with all men and the whole world.[123]

Conclusion

This brief survey has indicated the theological richness of a major current of Catholic thought. The point of departure for Scotist Christology and cosmology is the technical question of Christ's absolute primacy in the divine intentions. But from the Scotist resolution of this issue a whole series of theological affirmations follows. Christ is seen as Exemplar and Prototype of the cosmos, as Center and Mediator of the cosmos, as Final Cause, Scope, and Recapitulation of the cosmos. In such theologians as Peter Galatinus and Ambrogio Catarino Polito, significantly influenced by Scotus, one finds these themes focused into the explicit affirmation that Christ's glorified Body encompasses the totality of creation.

For Bérulle, another proponent of the Scotist thesis, the Incarnation shapes not only the history of salvation as more narrowly conceived, but the whole of cosmic history. The echo of the Fathers is discernible as Bérulle affirms that the Incarnation bestows on all creatures a new act of existence, consecrating the entire universe. All things are created through Christ and all converge in Christ. Christ's glorified Body is, as it were, a great new world which contains, renews, and fulfills the entire universe.

Blondelian thought subtly analyzes the openness of the natural to the supernatural, its aspiration for fulfillment in a higher order. Blondel affirms the organic unity of the whole universe and raises the epistemological and metaphysical issue of the substantial Bond as the ground for this unity. From the stance of faith Blondel finds the solution to this issue in Christ who is affirmed as ground and bond for the subsistence of all creatures. Blondel's affirmation of "pan-Christism," especially in his early period, carries with it a strong affirmation of Christ as the unifier of the divine plan, as recapitulator of the cosmos. Blondel explicitly aligns himself with the Scotist thesis of Christ's primacy, which he integrates with his notion of the organic union of the universe and Christ as the substantial bond of the whole.

If one views these thinkers in the wider context of Paul and the Fathers, one glimpses a theological current of cosmic Christology, discernible in the West as well as in the East, which provides through the ages an eloquent alternative to the non-cosmic, more constricted concepts of Christ. That is to say, in this context, that one begins to see Teilhard, no longer as innovator,[124] but as a quite traditional thinker bringing evolutionary science to the service of orthodox cosmic Christology.

CHAPTER FOUR

The Universe as Ordered Unity

Precisely because the cosmic Body model is so central an element in Teilhard's thought, it is profoundly interrelated with other key elements. Indeed, it draws these other elements together and assimilates them so that they become substantive for the model itself. One such element is the theme that the cosmos is a "unity," a "totum," an "organized whole," a "kind of gigantic 'atom,' " a "great organism."[1] Whole, organism, and Body so clearly interrelate and converge, that Teilhard uses the categories interchangeably — and cosmological vision of organic unity merges with Christological experience.[2]

TEILHARD'S VISION OF COSMIC UNITY

Teilhard was "an enthusiast of Unity,"[3] a man "driven by the passion for unity . . . to create unity where pluralistic fragmentation appears to reign supreme."[4] But if Teilhard was always in quest of unity, it was because he had, at the level of religious experience, already found it.[5] We have already discussed the mystical ground of Teilhard's theology of the universe, but it is well to recall here the intuitional character specifically of his theme of the organic unity of the universe.

Wildiers notes this deep origin of Teilhard's speculations:

> Undoubtedly, a salient feature of the picture which Teilhard . . . presented of the world is its closely knit internal coherence. What apparently gave it birth was a single initial intuition, which came to him at an early stage and attained greater depth and outreach as the years passed and as Teilhard tested it against his experience. He detected in the cosmos as a whole an awe-inspiring and thoroughgoing coherence, a profound organizational unity in which everything is bound up with everything and takes its *raison d'être* from its place within the whole.[6]

In treating of the organic unity of the cosmos Teilhard rarely resorts to speculative demonstration; he tries rather to evoke a certain religious insight or intuition, and he seems to know in advance that he will succeed in some cases and fail in others. He insists that he himself "can glimpse, or sense, a global Reality whose condition is that of being more necessary, more consistent, richer and more certain in its ways, than any of the particular things it embraces."[7] But "there are basically two types of mind, and only two: those who do not go beyond . . . perception of the multiple . . . and those for whom perception of this same multiple is necessarily completed in some unity."[8]

"Those who do not see, and those who do," Teilhard goes on to call these two groups. Seeing is, in fact, the key source for his theology of the universe. What he writes of *The Phenomenon of Man* applies to all his writings: "This work may be summed up as an attempt to *see* and *to make others see*. . . . Seeing. We might say that the whole of life lies in that verb—if not ultimately, at least essentially." [9]

What of those who reject the radical unity of the world, who opt for pluralism, who do not *see?* For Teilhard such an option is not just a subjective disposition; rather, he sees pluralism as negative and non-productive, whereas monism *affirms,* opens the way for action. Monism, moreover, is grounded objectively in the actual organic unity of the world and sustained subjectively by an illumination, an intuition of this unity.[10]

"It is precisely the value of this primordial intuition" which he feels sustains "the whole edifice of my belief."[11] Surely this sort of affirmation raises the whole thorny issue of the nature-grace relationship.[12] In this context, however, we want only to stress how fundamental for Teilhard is his commitment to the organic totality of the universe, and how directly this commitment carries him toward his basic theological-spiritual model of the cosmic Body of Christ.

Although Teilhard never provides a systematic treatment of his "cosmic sense" or intuition,[13] he does offer some powerful and suggestive reflections regarding its parallel with the intuition of love, and he insists that all men are endowed with this "faculty" or "sense":

> There is nothing astonishing, after all, in the existence of this "cosmic sense." Because he is endowed with sex, man undoubtedly has intuitions of love. Because he is an element, surely he must in some obscure way feel the attraction of the Universe. In fact, nothing in the vast and polymorphous domain of mysticism (religious, poetical, social, and scientific) can be explained without the hypothesis of such a faculty.[14]

If, as Teilhard goes on to maintain, one is monist by the very fact of being a man; if the "cosmic sense" is an "essential temperament" and a natural faculty, one may wonder why Teilhard invokes the need for *faith* and *conversion* for its exercise.

It could be said, in reply, that the "faith" he demands is of a wholly subordinate and natural kind, but such an interpretation (though it would obviate some thorny problems) would seem to be ruled out by the famous opening lines of *Comment je crois:*

> If, as a result of some interior revolution, I were to lose in succession my faith in Christ, my faith in a personal God, and my faith in Spirit, I feel that I should continue *to believe* invincibly *in the world.* The World (its value, its infallibility and its goodness) — that, when all is said and done, is the first, the last, and the only thing in which I believe. It is by this faith that I live. And it is to this faith, I feel, that at the moment of death, rising above all doubts, I shall surrender myself.

Needless to say, a great deal of ink has been expended upon the explanation of this passage.[15] Published attacks against the work began in Teilhard's own lifetime, and he himself addressed himself to its defense.[16] For present purposes, two points seem to emerge from a consideration of the text which concern us.

First, whatever else may be expressed or implied, the passage reveals how important the category of "universe" is for Teilhard — how profoundly rich, seminal, and organic is his cosmological conception. De Lubac, whose emphasis is always on the primacy of the supernatural and the Christological in Teilhard, acknowledges the prominence and breadth of the universe concept as revealed specifically by its organic character:

> To appreciate Teilhard's thought at this stage, it is not enough to state that the World in which the apologist expresses his faith, is incomparably richer and greater than that accepted by the unbeliever when both apologist and unbeliever set out on their common search. Nor is it sufficient to say that this World is richer and greater than the ordinary Universe of Science; or that this Universe of personal beings is something quite different from what most men generally understand by "Cosmos." The Teilhardian Universe . . . is richer and greater than that which the Christian himself generally envisages, when by a habitual methodical abstraction, he thinks only of the first result of the creation, adopting only the "natural" point of view of a philosophy of the spirit.[17]

The second point is that if such eulogies to faith in the universe are to be given the orthodox Christian interpretation Teilhard insists they deserve,[18] then the faith involved must be both open to and joined to a specifically "supernatural" faith in Christ's transforming action on the universe. But this is simply to repeat that Teilhard's concept of the universe's organic unity directly implies his model of the universe as Christ's cosmic Body. The latter model does not, then, stand alone; but neither does the former. The unity of the universe is ultimately the Pleroma of Christ.

As de Lubac astutely observes, the "primordial intuition" Teilhard speaks of is literally "primordial"—i.e., a starting point and not the whole picture. The faith he tries to evoke is faith "in its most wrapped-up form," and not a fully explicit Christian faith.[19] What Teilhard is trying to do is evoke in us a very fundamental intuition of the universe as Whole; only as we go on, with him, on the further steps to the completion of his vision, will this important starting point unfold and find its needed fulfillment in the vision of the universe as Christ's cosmic Body.

THE GREAT OPTION FOR THE WHOLE

Every man has a deep, mysterious sense of the Whole. But Teilhard sees this intuition as requiring an active response or commitment on man's part. We have seen him call this response "faith," but we must take care not to understand the "faith" in question in too intellectualist a way. Like Blondel, Teilhard stresses that it is a full, personal choice, of the sort that reorients one's whole life not only of thought but also of action.

This option is doubly vital in the context of Teilhard's evolutionary vision because man is seen not only as opting for a pre-existent unity, but also as summoned to achieve it — to carry cosmic unity forward towards its future consummation. This option therefore has crucial implications for every dimension (social and political, religious and economic) of human and thus cosmic existence:

> Pluralism or . . . monism? This is the ultimate choice, by way of which Mankind must finally be divided, knowing its own mind.
>
> In the view of the "pluralist" the world is moving in the direction of dispersal and therefore of growing autonomy of its separate elements. For each individual, the business, the duty and the interest of life consists in achieving, *in opposition to others,* his own utmost uniqueness and personal freedom. . . .
>
> But to the eyes of the "monist" the precise opposite is the case: nothing exists or finally matters except the Whole. For the elements of the world to become absorbed within themselves by separation from others, by isolation, is a fundamental error. . . .
>
> So the question can finally be posed . . . to fulfil ourselves individually by egotistically segregating ourselves from the mass; or to plunge resolutely into the stream of the whole in order to be incorporated therein.[20]

Notice how Teilhard assigns an anthropological dimension to the universe: man and world are not juxtaposed, but the latter finds its fulfillment in the former. At a still deeper level, the universe is Christic, however, and not merely anthropological. Man commits himself to the unity of the universe because the universe is man's and man himself must be one; but beyond that, the universe is Christ's, and Christ has made it one.[21]

The profoundly religious ground of Teilhard's thought is clearly in evidence even here, at what seems to be its most "natural" level. Otto might be describing Teilhard when he writes of the mysticism of "unifying vision" which "looks upon the world of things in its multiplicity, and in contrast to this leaps to an 'intuition' or a 'knowledge' [wherein] the One itself becomes the object of intuition as that which is superior and prior to the many. . . ."[22]

As Ramsey notes, the language used to recount this sort of religious experience is geared to evoking a cosmic insight and dedication:

> So we see religious commitment as a *total* commitment to a *whole* universe; something in relation to which argument has only a very odd function; its purpose being to tell such a tale as evokes the "insight," the "discernment" from which commitment follows as a response.[23]

Certainly Teilhard wishes ultimately to speak to the deeper religious level in man, but this is not to say that his assertion of a fundamental unity of the universe has meaning only on an ethereal level for an elite circle of illuminati. Teilhard's apostolate undoubtedly included a more empirical, concrete type of thinker, and he thus sought to vindicate in a great variety of ways the profound unity of the universe.

UNITY AS SCIENTIFIC-PHILOSOPHICAL PRESUPPOSITION

Teilhard suggests that the underlying unity of the universe may be not only a terminal insight of the matured thinker, but also a necessary starting point for the most elementary forms of reasoning. When a housewife, confronted by a puzzling quirk in her vacuum cleaner, spontaneously assumes that there is a natural cause — the cord poorly plugged in, or the nozzle clogged — she is but implicitly assuming that one phenomenon is decidedly related to another, that things don't just spontaneously "happen" in isolation. All of science is based upon the same "presupposition." Teilhard is emphatic:

> On the pain of being irreducible to scientific thought, everything must plunge its empirical roots into an indefinite past and into the entire area of its own present: this is the postulate which we find at the basis of all modern scientific research.[24]

And elsewhere,

> For the fundamental unity of the Universe and the inexorable interconnection and interaction of the cosmic elements . . . preclude any new being from emerging into our experience otherwise than in function of all the present and past states of the empirical world.[25]

Thus there is built into modern man's very thought processes a "demand for the unity of knowledge and being,"[26] a demand which requires and presupposes the internal nexus of all phenomena of the universe. But does this requirement pertain to the very structure of man's knowing process, or does it simply emerge in modern times with the advent, e.g., of evolutionism? Teilhard's primary concern is never with speculative epistemological issues, but he does at times suggest that the latter is the correct explanation:

> Formerly we were not too surprised by the sudden addition of atom to the cosmic mass, or by its sudden displacement across space. Today we no longer doubt that the existence of a molecule of hydrogen, for example, and its localization at a given point in the universe has required the immensity of a whole astral evolution. [27]

Wildiers vividly contrasts the newer organic conception with the former, more mechanistic one. "Science," he concludes, "has gradually made it more and more clear that all entities are interconnected, so that we can now see the world as mighty, organic whole, in which every single thing is related to everything else."[28]

This shift from mechanical to organic model is crucial, of course, for Teilhard's insight into the universe as cosmic Body of Christ. Were the universe a mere machine, Christ's receptive role might more easily be conceived as a liberation of Christian souls *from* such a mechanism (or, more positively, as a "lordship" of proprietorship over the machine viewed as a sort of stage-setting for man's spiritual drama).

But if the universe includes man and is understood in the light of the organism model, then the Incarnation must relate Christ to all things, and his redemptive recapitulation must encompass the whole cosmos. If man is to be integrally saved, then a universe must be saved. And if the universe is conceived of more as organism than as mechanism, Teilhard's cosmic Body model will appear not as theologically bizarre but rather as most relevant, appropriate, and fulfilling.

It is clear, in any case, that for Teilhard the organic unity of the universe appears as a necessary "presupposition" of modern science. But is it *only* a "presupposition"?

UNITY AS VERIFIED BY SCIENCE

Teilhard argues that this organic unity we have been talking about seems in our day to be "definitely accepted by the
human mind."[29] But what is the justification of this acceptance? Is it merely a matter of positing an arbitrary "presupposition" or hypothesis which somehow finds broad con-
sensus? Teilhard is convinced rather that this outlook has
been justified by the findings of science — and also by the
coherence it brings to human knowledge:

> We shall never abandon these concepts again, but explore them, on
> the contrary, to increasing depth because we have been both drawn
> and driven to them by the full force of human thought for many
> centuries; and also because, once they are accepted, reality is found to
> grow clearer and more orderly so far as the eye can see.[30]

Similarly, writing of evolution as "revealing the *irreversible
coherence* of all that exists," Teilhard considered the problem
of those who still rejected the concept:

> One might well become impatient or lose heart at the sight of so many
> minds (and not mediocre ones either) remaining today still closed to
> the idea of evolution, if the whole of history were not there to pledge
> to us that a truth once seen, even by a single mind, always ends up by
> imposing itself on the totality of human consciousness.[31]

Teilhard, then, regards the radical unity of the universe as
not only hypothesis but strongly verified by the physical and
biological sciences.[32] We cannot, of course, embark on a
technical investigation of these areas; but they are so essential to Teilhard's argument that we must at least advert to
some major aspects here.

The data of science verify his unified vision, Teilhard insists, in terms of both the "spatial vector" and the "temporal
vector" of the universe. Indeed, these two factors themselves
become conjoined in cosmic evolution: "Time and space are
organically joined again so as to weave, together, the Stuff of
the Universe."[33]

Regarding the "spatial vector," the realm of particular interest to the physicist, Teilhard stresses the physical interaction of the various elements of the universe and the
homogeneity of its structure. He speaks of a *fundamental*

unity which matter proclaims the more insistently as we try to split and pulverise it artificially; of a unity of *similarity* unveiled by chemical and physical descriptions of its particles; and of a unity of *homogeneity* in virtue of which any particle can be explained only in terms of all the others.[34]

Because of this unity of homogeneity and the interaction of all the elements, Teilhard treats of the sum of the matter in the universe as *one reality*—"Total Matter":

> Considered in its physical, concrete reality, the Stuff of the Universe cannot divide itself but, as a kind of gigantic "atom," it forms in its totality . . . the only real indivisible . . . the cosmos in which man finds himself caught up constitutes, by reason of the unimpeachable wholeness of its whole, a *system,* a *totum* and a *quantum*.[35]

Under the rubric of "system," Teilhard considers the universe in its aspect of a number of elements marvelously ordered, thoroughly interdependent in a hierarchical, structured whole. He insists that this "systematic" quality of the universe is attested by the "facts" of science: "The existence of 'System' in the world is at once obvious to every observer of nature," he asserts, and then he goes on to describe that "System" in some detail. "It is impossible to cut into this network," he concludes, "to isolate a portion without it becoming frayed and unravelled at all its edges." The only way we can take it is "as a whole, in one piece."[36]

But, Teilhard stresses, the universe is not constituted by the mere repetition of a single basic pattern on varying scales, such as Pascal had suggested.[37] There is, on the contrary, but one universe in which there obtains a continuously varied interrelation; the only key unit of the Whole is the Whole. He explicitly rejects the conception of matter by analogy with the crystal, observing that matter never repeats its different combinations.[38] Such vivid and emphatic reflections, well worth reading in full, are not without implication for anthropology (and thus for Christology); clearly even man's most spiritual functions are deeply rooted in the material, for "thought itself has need of a certain organic support, which is a function of certain physico-chemical conditions."[39]

Thus Teilhard wishes to substantiate his cosmological vision, at least in part, by recourse to the data of physics and chemistry. Competent judgment on this endeavor rests, of course, with thoroughly trained scientists who are also steeped in the rich complexities of Teilhard's unified vision. Many followers of Teilhard will insist with Coffy that the unity disclosed by science is "not a matter of imaginary vision or poetic dreams," but "a physical reality."[40] And indeed scientific progress seems all the more clearly to vindicate such a position, as a few examples serve to indicate.

Consider, first, the recently discovered "quasar" phenomena. Quasars are quasi-stellar radio sources so distant that their light and radio waves seem to have taken billions of years to reach us. Thus in viewing them we may be looking back in time perhaps to the infancy of the universe, studying phenomena at a very remote distance in the cosmos.[41]

Teilhard argues, in the second place, that the same basic physical elements and forces obtain throughout the universe. The prominent physicist Robert Jastrow corroborates this claim, observing that

> it is remarkable that all objects in the universe, from the smallest nucleus to the largest galaxy, are held together by only three fundamental forces—a nuclear force, the force of electromagnetism, and the force of gravity.[42]

"All objects in the universe hold together", he continues, according to certain constant forces; and they are built up by the same elements.[43] And since "each atom exerts a small gravitational attraction on its neighbor," the universe is a web of interaction and influence at the fundamental level of its elements.[44]

Even though a scientist might be puzzled by some of Teilhard's more poetic phrases, therefore, he would certainly agree that the universe is best conceived as woven together into a single extraordinary whole. Perhaps most of us in our day-to-day lives tend to look upon the various objects of our experience as thoroughly individual and juxtaposed. The world of physics, as well as the thought of Teilhard, invites us to a deeper view.

UNITY AS EVOLUTIONAL

From the foregoing discussion of the "spatial" dimension, let us turn to Teilhard's much more emphatic insistence on the temporal, evolutive dimension. This is, as Crespy observes, the "first of the great Teilhardian insights," that *"Time is the vector along which a world organizes itself."*[45]

In fact, the temporal and spatial vectors are not, for Teilhard, juxtaposed; they are brought together by the force of cosmic evolution into the organic totality:

> The least molecule is, in nature and in position, a function of the whole sidereal process, and the least of the protozoa is structurally so knit into the web of life that its existence cannot be hypothetically annihilated without *ipso facto* undoing the whole network of the biosphere. *The distribution, succession, and solidarity of objects are born from their concrescence in a common genesis.* Time and space are organically joined again so as to weave, together, the Stuff of the Universe.[46]

This insight sums up, for Teilhard, not only his own vision but also what he sees as the new consciousness of mankind:

> A first point which emerges for me with a forcefulness that I cannot even dream of questioning, is that the Unity of the World is by its nature dynamic or evolutive. Here I am simply meeting in myself . . . the discovery of Duration which for the last century has so profoundly been modifying mankind's former consciousness of the Universe. Besides space, so staggering to Pascal, we now have time—not a container-time in which years are stored, but an organic time which is measured by the development of global reality. We used to look upon ourselves and the things around us as "points" closed in on themselves. We now see beings as threadless fibers, woven into a universal process. . . . Through its history, every being is co-extensive with the whole of duration; and its ontogenesis is no more than the infinitesimal element of a cosmogenesis in which is ultimately expressed the individuality—the face, we might say—of the Universe.[47]

Teilhard is looking beyond the immediate descent of living species, then, to the broader scale of the evolving course of the universe. Such a conception achieves the organic totalization of all things not on a spatial plane but in terms of cosmic past and cosmic future.

Teilhard understands his concept of cosmic, evolutionary cohesion to be well grounded, moreover, in scientific data.[48] He is proposing not only a "mystical intuition," not only a working presupposition, but a scientific concept which he feels can claim significant scientific verification. Not that all scientists (particularly in his day) would agree; not that many particular points of difference would not arise. But in its basic affirmation of evolutionary cohesion on a cosmic scale, Teilhard's position does accord with that of most scientists today. As Jastrow notes, "a single thread of evidence runs from the atom and the nucleus through the formation of stars and planets to the complexities of the living organism." After a vivid and detailed account of cosmic evolution, he concludes that "man's history began billions of years before the solar system itself was formed; it began in a swirling cloud of primordial hydrogen."[49]

The common sense perspective which fragments the universe into a disparate collection of self-enclosed entities thus clashes as much with the scientific world-view as it does with Teilhard's vision. "The more one heeds the invitations to analyze urged on one by contemporary thought and science," Teilhard observes,

> the more one feels imprisoned in the network of cosmic inter-relationships. Through criticism of knowledge, the subject becomes continually more closely identified with the most distant reaches of a Universe which it can know only by becoming to some degree one body with it. Through biology . . . the living being becomes more and more in series with the whole web of the biosphere. Through physics, a boundless homogeneity and solidarity is brought to light in the layers of matter. "Everyting holds together." Expressed in this elementary form, faith in the World does not differ noticeably from the acceptance of a scientific truth.[50]

A PHILOSOPHY OF COSMIC UNITY

Of course it is not just on the level of science that Teilhard advances his concept of the universe as a cohesive, dynamic Whole. He also proposes a comprehensive, though not technically elaborated, "philosophy of creative union."[51] In considering the vast spectrum of philosophical issues, he seeks "to reduce everything to the notion of union,"[52] and he aspires thereby to transcend the traditional antinomies:

> Thus those innumerable difficulties vanish which every philosophy comes up against that tries to reconstruct the world from isolated elements . . . instead of affirming the principle of the fundamental and substantial unity of the Universe.[53]

Teilhard sought the ultimate ground for his "metaphysics of union"[54] in the unification of the Divine Persons. In trinitarian theology, he observes, we begin by presupposing God's existence as self-sufficient "supreme Being." But for God to exist in total independence as origin and goal of everything else,

> it must be further assumed (in conformity with the data of revelation) . . . that this Center [God] is constituted by internal trinitarian relations. In this way, the ontological principle upon which our metaphysics is based is seen to hold good even at the most profound and indeed primordial level of being: God himself, in a rigorously real sense, exists only through a process of self-unification.[55]

It cannot be our purpose here to consider the problematic of founding a "metaphysics" on trinitarian doctrine, or of deducing from an "ontology" the distinction of divine Persons. If such a scheme seems to overemphasize God's "self-unification" at the expense of the distinction of Persons – a tendency Eastern theologians perceive in Western theology generally[56] – it should be noted that Teilhard is discussing, not precisely the unity of the divine nature, but rather the dynamic "self-unification" of the Persons' inner life, a notion which perhaps finds parallel in the rich Eastern theme of circumincession.[57]

The central Teilhardian theme that "union differentiates" receives a particularly profound elucidation in this conception of the triune Godhead, "archetype of creation."[58] New cogency is imparted to the truth that the unity of the universe heightens rather than dissolves the unique identities of the elements. Teilhard's philosophy of the unity of the universe is, at any rate, deeply and solidly rooted "at the most profound and indeed primordial level of being." If the "philosophy of creative union" is ultimately trinitarian; if the unification of the universe is but an image of the primordial unification of the Trinity, this can only be because there intercedes the key mediating archetype of the Body of Christ.[59] The organic unity of the cosmos is fundamentally Christic:

> The reader will have already seen for some time that the philosophy of creative union is simply the development, the generalization, the extension to the entire Universe of what the Church teaches us concerning the growth of Christ. *It is the Universe conceived in function*

of the notion of the mystical Body. It was in reflecting upon the mystical Body that I discovered the theory of creative union, and it is only so that it can be understood: by striving to love and hold Christ in all things.[60]

So Teilhard's organic cosmology is rooted in a Christology as well as a trinitarian theology. It is also buttressed with his own peculiar ontology of being as unity, nothingness as disunity:

Of every being we know it is true to say that the more it is divided, the less existence it has.... By dispersing, a being is annihilated. It vanishes in plurality....

From all eternity God saw beneath his feet the scattered shadow of his Unity.... It was then that the superabundant Unity of life engaged, through the creation, in battle with the non-existing Multiple.... *So far as we can see, to create is to condense,* concentrate, organize — *to unify.*[61]

Here two points seem to emerge which are both compelling and unambiguous.

First, for a universe dynamically evolving, the mystery of creation is more correctly formulated as a continuing process, than as an act of the past which once for all brought into existence a variety of creatures substantially the same as today. That is, the world is best seen as "in process of being created through a gradual unification of multiplicity."[62]

Secondly, the concept of being is intimately bound up with that of unity. Teilhard's is a position which Thomas Aquinas would certainly have endorsed: *ens et unum convertuntur* — being and the one are interchangeable.[63] But given an evolutionary universe, Teilhard felt that this fundamental metaphysical truth needed a correspondingly dynamic expression: the more elements *become* unified in the course of their development, the more they attain, as it were, to being.

This is a basic principle of Teilhard's implicit ontology: the greater the organic unity, the fuller the being:

Creative union is the theory that accepts this proposition: in the present evolutionary phase of the Cosmos (the only phase known to us), everything happens as though the One were formed by successive unifications of the Multiple — and as though the One were more perfect in direct proportion to its capacity to center within itself in a more perfect way a larger multiplicity.

Then Teilhard spontaneously invokes the body-soul model to explicate his ontology:

> For the elements grouped together by the soul into the body (and by that very fact raised to a higher level of being)... "to be more is to be more fully united with more." For the soul itself, the principle of unity [is]... "to be more is more fully to unite more." For both, to receive or to communicate union is to undergo the creative influence of God... "who creates by uniting."[64]

This has interesting implications for Teilhard's theological cosmology and his Christology. If the order of grace does not destroy, but fulfills that of nature; if the universe is destined to attain a full Christian realization, then it must be shaped into a Whole, an organic union in Christ. On the Christ-ological side, if Christ's Body is to be totally fulfilled; if it is not to appear constricted and deficient in the cosmic context, then it must contain a maximum of cosmic elements—*plus esse est plura unire*.

Teilhard's theology of the cosmic Body springs organically out of his basic concept of being as maximum dynamic unity, and of truth as maximum universal coherence:

> ... the more I have thought about the magnificent cosmic attributes lavished by St. Paul on the risen Christ... the more clearly have I realized that Christianity takes on its full value only when extended (as I find it rewarding to do) to cosmic dimensions.... The more I think about it, the less I can see any criterion for truth other than the establishment of a growing maximum of universal coherence. Such an achievement has something *objective* about it, going beyond the effects of temperament.[65]

In the Teilhardian philosophical vision, being and truth thus find their elucidation through the categories of union and wholeness. The vision is profoundly affirmative. As the "greater," the "Whole," is vindicated, there is also asserted the primacy of supreme consciousness within that "Whole":

> Before embarking on a synthetic exposition of the philosophy that supports and gives organic form to the building up of my moral and religious constructions, it may be well to bring out a number of fundamental principles or postulates in which can be seen the "spirit" in which my representation of the Universe has been conceived and in which it has developed.

1. *The primacy of consciousness*

Logically and psychologically, the first of these principles is the profound conviction that being is good: in other words,

    a. that it is better to be than not to be;

    b. that it is better to be more than to be less.

If we accept as an auxiliary principle that "complete" being is conscious being, then we may express this principle in a clearer and more practical form, as follows:

    a. that it is better to be conscious than not to be conscious.

    b. that it is better to be more conscious than less conscious.[66]

We have here the great Teilhardian vision of hierarchical levels in the ascending, dynamic Whole: "The Universe organizes itself in a single, grand progression, somewhat untidy no doubt, but on the whole clear in its orientation, ascending from the most rudimentary atom to the highest form of living things."[67]

This evolutionary dynamic has a direction, of course,[68] and a scale is provided for assessing the relative value of the different elements of the universe. This scale is constituted by rating the degree of bio-chemical complexity of the various elements,[69] which has a "relationship of concomitance"[70] to the level of consciousness attainable. And this coefficient of complexity "enables us to establish, among the natural units which it has helped us to 'identify' and isolate, a system of classification that is . . . natural and universal."[71]

Teilhard's "law of complexity-consciousness" has been subjected to much analysis and evaluation.[72] For present purposes it suffices to note that the principle posits a universe that is ordered and hierarchical. It affirms, moreover, that the phenomena of life and consciousness do not stand in contradiction to the rest of creation but rather rise out of a general potency of the Whole and lead to its more rigorous centration. Life, as Smulders observes,

becomes the supreme form of the fabric of the cosmos, in which a fundamental law [that of] . . . interiorizing complexification, manifests itself at its utmost pitch with unrivalled clarity. . . . For life, especially human life, tinged as it is with both the material and the spiritual, is not an anomaly in the fabric of the cosmos; it is rather the actualization and crown of a fundamental property of that whole fabric, namely, the tendency to interiorizing complexification.[73]

If man were seen as simply an alien in this world; if human consciousness were conceived as an anomaly for the cosmos, then the organic wholeness of the universe and its "physical" unification in Christ would appear as thoroughly bizarre concepts. But if man and consciousness are seen as actualizing and unifying fundamental potencies of the universe as such, then the notion of a further, decisive centration of the humanized universe in Christ appears as an appropriate theological fulfillment of the whole of creation.

How is the universe actuated, fulfilled, rendered whole? In the passage just cited we see the image of a unifying *fabric;* to this is often added the complementary, equally basic image of a unifying *center.* And since evolution is conceived as convergent — as conic — an additional model of totalization is proposed: that of a unifying *apex.* Thus when Teilhard proposes his vision of cosmic unity, he is arguing that the dynamic thrust of the Whole is rendered cohesive by a unifying *fabric, center,* and *apex.*

In this manner, the universe is totalized by human consciousness, which binds together, centers, and crowns the whole thrust of cosmic evolution. But humanity can fulfill this totalizing function only in an imperfect, relative, and proximate way, for men themselves must be brought together, must find a common center, must seek a common goal. Converging evolution reaches a key new threshold in mankind, it is true; but mankind is simply, in Gray's perceptive phrase, "a new multiplicity to be unified." Mankind is "a new multiplicity in search of unity, a new matter in search of spirit, a new body in search of a soul."[74]

Of course it is Christ whom Teilhard affirms as the definitive unifier of the cosmos. Utilizing a great variety of models, Teilhard proposes Christ as cosmic center and milieu, as quasi-formal cause, as soul of the universe, as its substantial bond, its Omega, its head, etc. The universe is thus rendered organically unified in Christ. A fuller examination of the Christological dimensions of the universe will be offered in the next chapter. But one cannot neatly compartmentalize Teilhard's thought, and we must note here that when Teilhard is sketching his philosophy of creative union, he is already proposing a cosmos that is radically anthropological and Christological — a universe which is the Body of Christ: "The philosophy of creative union is simply . . . *the philosophy of the Universe conceived in function of the notion of the mystical Body.*"[75] For "the full significance of the theory of creative union is to be found in the doctrine of the Body of Christ."[76]

CHAPTER FIVE

The Universe As Intrinsically Christic

The cosmic Body model, as we have seen, assimilates and fulfills the key Teilhardian theme of the universe as ordered unity. Another even more prominent theme, that of the universe as intrinsically Christic, also finds its focus in the cosmic Body model, and thus it completes the theme of unity: the universe becomes organic whole specifically in Christ.

Teilhard repeatedly affirms that Christ binds the universe to himself not by mere juridical title or extrinsic lordship, but rather intrinsically, "physically," "ontologically." Creation occurs in Christ and for Christ, who exercises exemplary and even quasi-formal causality over the whole. By his Incarnation, Jesus decisively unifies and assimilates the entire cosmos. The Redemption extends in its efficacy beyond individual souls to the universe itself, even more decisively unifying it, "super-creating" it in Christ. Creation, Incarnation, Redemption: Teilhard directly applies all three dimensions of the Christian mystery to the universe, thus investing them with cosmic scope and binding the universe intrinsically to Christ.[1]

The cosmic Body model expresses this unified, intrinsically Christic character of the universe in a particularly striking manner, but other themes such as Christ the "animator," the "form" and "head" of the universe, also underline, each with its own emphasis, the intrinsically Christic character of the universe. As we have observed, these themes have been analyzed frequently for their specifically Christological significance; but they must also be studied as theology of the universe. Cosmic Christology implies Christic cosmology: "My road ahead seems clearly marked out; it is a matter not of superimposing Christ on the World but of 'panChristising' the Universe."[2]

Although Teilhard never provides a fully elaborated systematic theology of the universe in its Christic dimension, he does offer a suggestive sketch of many elements of such a theology. This sketch constitutes the speculative, abstract level which is nourished and concretized by his key model of Christ's cosmic Body.

THE UNIVERSE AS CREATED IN CHRIST

Teilhard was always deeply interested in the mystery of creation. In 1918, he wrote:

> I've also felt that the problem of creation, looked at not in its present (evolutive) phase but in its first (involutive), is taking on increasing importance in my mind. What is the origin of the lower multiple? What "need" is filled by the fundamental fragmentation of being—driven from its source before returning to it? Until this problem is more or less coherently cleared up, one can't, I think, understand the worth of souls and the value of the Incarnation.[3]

The ambiguous and problematic character of Teilhard's thought on creation is well known. Some have charged that he falsely presents matter as "eternal in itself"[4] and the creative process as a shaping by God of pre-existing realities, like a struggle "between the One and the multiple . . . reminiscent of those Babylonian cosmologies. . . ."[5] Some decry what appears to them as necessitarianism,[6] but others argue for the "essential orthodoxy, if not always the mode of expression, of Teilhard's argument,"[7] and they cite Teilhard's "oft-repeated intention to remain strictly within the framework of the Christian doctrine of creation. . . ."[8] Our interest in this intricate web of problems is limited to determining features of relevance to Teilhard's basic commitment to the Christic dimension of the universe.

The key issue for Teilhard in analyzing the creative act is precisely the *interconnection* or relationship between God and the world. He wants to get at that relationship in a way that transcends the traditional category of efficient causality.[9] He wants, as he put it, prayerfully to examine "the zone *where God and the cosmos meet*,"[10] and this "zone" is the cosmic Body of Christ.

A moment ago reference was made to alleged necessitarianism in Teilhard. It is true that he does not consider creation to be an arbitrary whim—a matter of sheer indifference to God. He does see God as "needing" creation in the sense that it mysteriously completes the Pleroma or Body of Christ.[11] But the "necessity" involved is the same as that involved in traditional Scotist theology: given that God wants his "masterpiece" (the Incarnate Word), a universe is needed as context. As Teilhard expresses it, in willing Christ, God willed an entire universe.[12]

Some indication has also been given in the preceding chapter of the authentically Pauline character of this theme of creation in Christ. Recent and contemporary exegetes differ in the precise weight each attaches to each of the various categories they use to express the relation of Jesus Christ to the totality of creation. Thus Cerfaux seems to stress both Christ's role as goal, "knitting together" the whole universe,[13] and Christ's secondary efficient causality, attributed to him precisely as the God-*man*.[14] Huby seeks something more emphatic than exemplary causality and finds it in "centrality"—Christ is for him "the supreme center of unity, harmony, and cohesion."[15] But it is generally the exegetes and theologians of the Scotist school who have most consistently stressed what they consider the authentically Pauline doctrine of Christ's absolute primacy, embracing a whole network of causal relationships placing the cosmos in dependence upon the Incarnate Word.

This profound theme of the Christic dimension of creation, though richly developed by the Eastern Fathers,[16] did not receive its full vindication in scholastic theology with the exception of such theological currents as the Franciscan, "where creation in Christ gained its place of special honor."[17]

Teilhard himself, of course, explicitly affirms that the universe is created in and through Christ, and he vindicates his position by an appeal to scripture:

I need only refer to the long series of Johannine—and still more Pauline—texts in which the physical supremacy of Christ [is asserted] over the Universe. I cannot quote them all here, but they come down to these two essential affirmations: "In eo omnia constant" (Col. 1:17), and "Ipse est qui replet omnia" (Col. 2:10; cf. Eph. 4:9) from which it follows that "Omnia in omnibus Christus" (Col. 3:11)—the very definition of omega.[18]

Teilhard clearly feels spontaneously drawn to the thesis of the Christic dimension of the universe because of his decisive pan-Christism and also because of his vivid sense that all things are radically interconnected in an organic unity. Far from being a lately arrived "propriétaire,"[19] Christ is the heart and center and key for the whole creation:

> This is the point we must bear in mind: in no case could the Cosmos be conceived and realized, without a supreme centre of spiritual consistence. . . . What gives the World its "gratuitous" character is precisely that the position of universal Centre has not been given to any supreme intermediary between God and the Universe, but has been occupied by the Divinity himself. . . . Since the Pauline Christ (the great Christ of the mystics) coincides with the universal term, omega, adumbrated by our philosophy—the grandest and most necessary attribute we can ascribe to him is that of exercising a supreme physical influence on every cosmic reality without exception.[20]

The pervasive and mutually complementary themes of the universe requiring a Christ for its unification and a Christ requiring a universe to assimilate, are here presented in the key of creational theology:

> God did not will individually (nor could he have constructed as though they were separate bits) the sun, the earth, plants, or Man. He willed his Christ; and in order to have his Christ, he had to create the spiritual world, and man in particular, upon which Christ might germinate; and to have man, he had to launch the vast process of organic life (which, accordingly, is not a superfluity but an essential organ of the World); and the birth of that organic life called for the entire cosmic turbulence.[21]

Also indicated in these lines is Teilhard's conception of creation as, not a once-for-all act by which God once posited things in a finalized form, but a dynamic, ongoing process. Creation, for Teilhard is certainly an "evolutive" process,

> but God brings about real novelty or "creation" at the level of each new union. Where there is no union at all there is nothing. Through union God brings his creation into being. Through the continuing process of evolution, God is bringing his creation to ever higher states of being.[22]

So Teilhard calls his brand of creationism an "evolutionary type,"[23] according to which "to create, even for omnipotence, should not be understood by us as an instantaneous act, but as a process or act of synthesis. . . ."[24] It is by uniting, by synthesizing, that God creates; and Christ is the key to the *mode* of this unification. This is all spelled out through a series of interlocking models which illumine from various angles Christ's unifying function: Christ is Omega, point of convergence, and magnetic, unifying pole for the universe; he is center and axis for the universe; and he is the soul or substantial Bond of the universe.

Christ is not "structurally detached" from creation, whose existence would be seen as decreed only consequently upon sin; nor is he a mere extrinsic exemplar. He is the very shape and ultimate substance of creation, "a kind of 'formal' cause" of creation.[25] "Christogenesis . . . is itself the soul of universal cosmogenesis,"[26] and thus creation "becomes wholly Christological in character."[27]

This Christocentric theology of creation represents to a significant extent a reaction against the manualistic theology of Teilhard's day,[28] and Teilhard has no hesitation in contrasting the two:

> The learned may smile, or be angered, to hear us speak of progress. They may smugly enumerate the scandals of the present day, or argue about original sin, to prove that nothing good can come from the Earth. We may disregard these pessimists, who seem never to have questioned history, or reason, or their own hearts. But have they the faintest suspicion, these men, that their scepticism will end logically in making the World unintelligible, and in destroying our capacity to act?[29]

Frequently Teilhard links this pessimism explicitly to a theological position "still currently presented in pious books, in sermons, and even in seminary teaching," noting that this theology is characterized by "a general almost Manichean mistrust of anything material. . . ."[30] Teilhard's own theology of original sin, which early occasioned great difficulty with the authorities in Rome,[31] avoids any such denigration of the positive and Christic value of the universe. In contrast to the manualists, Teilhard uses the doctrine of original sin to argue to Christ's cosmic efficacy and to the organic unity of the universe in Christ. This early formulation of his argument is worth citing in full:

1. *If Christ is to be truly universal,* the Redemption, and hence the Fall, must extend to the whole Universe. Original sin accordingly takes on a *cosmic nature* that tradition has always accorded to it, but which, in view of the new dimensions we recognize in our Universe, obliges us radically to restate the historical representation of that sin and the too purely juridical way in which we commonly describe its being passed on.

2. If it is possible for the Universe to have been affected as one whole by an accident that occurred in certain souls, then its coherence *"in unitate materiae et in unitate spiritus"* must be infinitely greater than we used generally to admit. *To conform to the evidence of dogma,* the World can no longer be an agglomeration of juxtaposed objects: we must recognize it as one great Whole, welded together and evolving organically. The theoreticians of Christianity will have to overhaul the whole metaphysics of the One and the Multiple, if we wish our philosophy to meet the demands of our theology.

3. If Christ is universal (if, in other words, he is gradually consummated from all created things) it follows that his kingdom, in its essence, goes beyond the domain of the life that is, in a strict sense, called supernatural. . . .

4. If this work, finally, of Christ's fulfillment is to have a meaning, is to be worth what it has cost God, the mysterious *Compound* formed by Christ and the Universe (by the Universe centred on Christ) must have a specific and unique value. . . . At a time when human thought is coming to recognize the Cosmos as a Whole *per se,* it would be well to devote some thought to the relationship that unites that Whole to God. We need not look far for an answer: creation by love, outward glory. But is this all that is contained in the deposit of revelation?[32]

This complex and not always tightly reasoned text demonstrates at least that for Teilhard original sin actually vindicates rather than precludes the assertion of the universe's Christic dimension.

Teilhard's identification of creation with unification, insufficiently stressed by most commentators, is actually close to the heart of his whole outlook.[33] But this makes it all the more important that we realize the ulterior, *Christic,* foundation of this theory of creative union. To create is to unite, and the fundamental bond of union for creation is

Christ. Thus the process of creation is simply the continuing "act of forming and consummating Christ" who "sur-animates the world."[34] The forces of creation, including man in co-operation with the Creator, are working to isolate certain energies of disintegration and to advance the forces of union, "of which the progressive sublimation, *in Christo Jesu,* is, for the Creator, the fundamental operation taking place." Of course the locus for this creative unification is the *Body* of Christ. Using the obviously appropriate metaphor of the tree (which abounds in his writings), Teilhard goes on to stress the organic character of the unification:

> And the task of the Body of Christ, living in his faithful, is patiently to sort out those heavenly forces—to extract, witout letting any of it be lost, that chosen substance. Little by little, we may rest assured, the work is being done. Thanks to the multitude of individuals and vocations, the Spirit of God insinuates itself everywhere and is everywhere at work. It is the great tree . . . whose sunlit branches refine and turn to flowers the sap extracted by the humblest of its roots.[35]

THE COSMIC IMPLICATIONS OF THE INCARNATION

It is only to be expected that Teilhard would link his theme of the intrinsically Christic universe with the mystery of the Incarnation itself:

> Whereas the concept "Body of Christ" is always linked in Paul's mind to Christ's redemptive death and Resurrection and only implicitly to the Incarnation, the same concept in Teilhard is almost synonymous with the Incarnation and hence closer to the Greek Fathers, whose theology developed at length the Incarnation's role in God's plan of salvation. It is because of this difference in emphasis that Teilhard finds it quite easy to reach the cosmos directly through "Body of Christ" without mention of the Church at all.[36]

If "Incarnation" is almost synonymous with "Body of Christ" for Teilhard, it is also deeply interrelated with the theme of creation itself—an interrelation resulting from Teilhard's Scotist stress on creation in Christ. So Teilhard can consider the two mysteries as almost interchangeable, as when he writes of the Eucharist that "through it passes directly the axis of the Incarnation, that is to say the axis of creation."[37] More precisely, Teilhard sees the "incarnation of the Word as the final term of the process of creation," so that one ongoing development is marked by the decisive water-shed of the Incarnation.

Using yet another model, "part-Whole," Teilhard suggests that the Incarnation is but one aspect of the same total mystery denoted by the term "creation": "Like the Creation (of which it is the visible aspect) the Incarnation is an act coextensive with the duration of the World."[38]

Close relationship with the Incarnation implies, of course, equally intimate connection with the Redemption. Indeed, the Redemption of creation has already begun with the Incarnation:

> The Universe is rent asunder; it suffers a painful cleavage at the heart of each of its monads, as the Flesh of Christ is born and grows. Like the work of Creation, which it redeems and surpasses, the Incarnation, so desired of man, is an awe-inspiring operation. It is achieved through blood.[39]

Like St. John and the Greek Fathers, Teilhard thus sees the Incarnation as the initiation of cosmic Redemption; for the Incarnation represents not just the union of one isolated human nature with the Word but rather a cosmic event whereby, through the sacred humanity of Christ, the whole of creation finds its center, its life and light.

It follows that if there are negative cosmic repercussions of original sin (which Teilhard would be the last to deny) the world is *not* on that account to be seen as fundamentally deformed. The decisive unifying force of the Incarnation more than compensates for sin's divisive havoc and makes creation a positive asset for the spiritual life:

> Of its nature, and as a result of original sin, it is true that matter represents a perpetual impulse towards failure. But by nature too, and as a result of the Incarnation, it contains the spur or the allurement to be our accomplice towards heightened being, and this counter-balances and even dominates the *fomes peccati.*[40]

The entire universe is thus invested with a sort of sacramental quality; like a powerful magnetic force, the incarnate Word pulls it into saving cohesion:

> *The Divine Magnetism:* Christ's primordial role is to draw to himself all that, before him, moved at random. . . . For the Universe to subsist,

even in its natural evolution, it was necessary above all that the dynamic soul of one and the same vigorous impetus should again be instilled into men. God chose the love of his incarnate Son as the prime mover of the restored Universe.[41]

This theology of a Christic universe leads quite spontaneously into the concrete model of Christ's cosmic Body; and this logic implies that the universe has no merely "natural" reality, unity or finality:

> ... the Incarnation so completely *recast* the Universe in the supernatural that, *in concrete fact,* we can no longer ask, or imagine, towards what Centre the elements of this World, had they not been raised up by grace, would have gravitated.
>
> ... the philosophy of creative union is simply the development— generalization, extension to the Universe—of what the Church teaches us about the growth of Christ. *It is the philosophy of the Universe expressed in terms of the notion of mystical Body.*[42]

Given that the Incarnation does, in Teilhard's view, affect the entire universe, the problem then arises of explaining how this influence is to be understood. We have just seen that by the image of a magnetic force Teilhard vivifies the idea that Christ is the one "final cause" organizing and orienting the whole. But he also uses images of a more organic, biological character—and a different causal framework as well: that of formal causality—to clarify Christ's relationship to the universe:

> Is the kingdom of God a big family? Yes, in a sense it is. But in another sense it is a prodigious biological operation—that of the Redeeming Incarnation.
>
> As early as in St. Paul and St. John we read that to create, to fulfil and to purify the World is, for God, to unify it by uniting it organically with himself. How does he unify it? By partially immersing himself in things, by becoming "element," and then, from this point of vantage of the heart of matter, assuming the control and leadership of what we now call evolution.[43]

Here Christ is likened, not simply to a geometrical center for a circle of cosmic dimensions, nor to a magnetic pole for a universal array of filings, but (so as to communicate better the full force of the Christic-cosmic unity) as a "prodigious biological operation."

In this biological operation, Teilhard goes on to say, Christ "superanimates" the whole until the final consummation, when "he will close in upon himself and his conquests" for the decisive union. "Superanimation," with its cluster of terms such as "form," "soul," and "animator," is actually subordinate to the dominant organic image of grafting, used, e.g., in his description of the Incarnation as "an operation . . . to graft the Person of God into the human cosmos. . . ."[44] Another image subordinated to this same grafting-metaphor is that of "assimilation": "From the cosmic element into which he inserts himself," Teilhard explains, "the Word acts to subjugate all else and assimilate it to himself."[45]

The divine "Graft" means the transformation, the divinization, not just of mankind but of the entire cosmos:

> I see your Flesh extend throughout the entire Universe, there to be mingled with it and so extract from it all the elements that can be made to serve your purpose. . . .
> *To bring Christ, by virtue of a specifically organic connexion, to the heart of Realities that are esteemed the most dangerous, the most natural, the most pagan — in that you have my gospel and my mission. . . .*[46]

This rich and mystical passage, in the course of which Teilhard also speaks of showing "the life of the Lord Jesus flowing through all things — the true Soul of the World," reveals a veritable cluster of key organic models. Christ's *Body* is truly cosmic — his *flesh* extends throughout the entire universe, because by his Incarnation he has established a *specifically organic connexion* with the totality of creation, so that there is revealed *the life of the Lord Jesus flowing through all things*.

Teilhard wants this physical, organic character duly acknowledged, moreover, and all extrinsicism decisively repudiated. He decries the way in which "the organic side of the Incarnation, and in consequence its physical presuppositions or conditions, were relegated to the background," and insists that Christ is "physically and literally *He who fills all things* . . . the organic principle of . . . [the whole] harmonizing process," so that the cosmos is "animated by his form."[47]

Through his Incarnation, Christ thus "made Himself in some way . . . what would constitute a 'soul of the World.' "[48] Certainly Teilhard is aware of the dangers involved in the use of these categories,[49] but he is not a timid thinker, and the whole thrust of his thought leads him to affirm that

> even before the Incarnation became a fact, the whole history of the Universe (in virtue of a pre-action of the humanity of Christ, mysterious, but yet known to us through revelation) is the history of a progressive information of the Universe by Christ.[50]

This same almost reckless insistence on intrinsic organicism as against extrinsicism, was noted above in our analysis of Teilhard's theology of creation. It is nonetheless important to repeat it here in, as it were, the incarnational key: Christ truly enters into the universe in the Incarnation, becoming not merely its "lord" by arbitrary divine decree, but rather its very center, head, "form."

"Form." Why this preoccupation with formal causality? Teilhard was naturally drawn to the causality categories he knew from his manualist training. Efficient causality, while needed as a partial answer, does not suffice because "it introduces between [participated and uncreated Being] an *exteriority* which is surely exaggerated."[51] Exemplary causality in the usual strict sense tends to suggest a model *distinct from* what is patterned upon it.[52] And material causality, while truly intrinsic, cannot apply here, since Christ's function "is to be not a quasi-matter, a plastic or informable element, an agent of absorption, but a quasi-Soul, a plasmatic or informing element, a force of determination."[53] Teilhard is left, then, with formal causality, which is both intrinsic and the principle of actualization.

The causality in question is not merely that of a form taken in the most general sense, but rather that of the *soul,* the form of *living* beings. In Aristotelian scholasticism, the soul not only actuates, but also animates the living being. So for Teilhard Christ actualizes, unifies, and animates the cosmic Whole as its "soul."

There is still another dimension to the Aristotelian notion of form or soul which Teilhard most felicitously exploits: the form is also the intrinsic final cause or goal. True, a final cause can be purely extrinsic and its influence can consist "in nothing more than its being a good which is the term of appetite or desire."[54] But this is not the sort of finality Teilhard attributes to Jesus Christ:

> Let us, for brevity's sake, give the name of omega to the upper cosmic term disclosed by creative union. All that I shall have to say about it may be reduced to three points:
> A. The revealed Christ is identical with omega.
> B. It is inasmuch as He is omega that He is seen to be attainable and inevitably present in all things.
> C. And finally it was in order that He might become omega that it was necessary for Him, through the travail of the Incarnation, to conquer and animate the Universe.[55]

The form of man, for Aristotle, not only makes John Smith a human being; it directs all John's development *from within* towards his attainment of full human stature. So the important Teilhardian model of Christ as Omega, magnetic pole, or universal goal is not at all in conflict with the complementary stress on Christ as quasi-Soul. On the contrary, intrinsic finality is an important facet of formal causality itself which deserves the explicit emphasis Teilhard gives it.

Still, it is formal causality which dominates; with all due reservations made, "the word that comes nearest to a satisfactory definition of the universal influx of Jesus Christ, the Centre of the World, is 'information.' "[56] As we have seen, Teilhard is sometimes careful to qualify his affirmation of formal causality. The question thus arises now, does such a qualification as "quasi" in the phrase "quasi-formal" empty his affirmation of all real content and literal force? In an analogous case, Karl Rahner insists that his description of created grace as a "quasi-formal causality of God himself upon the created spirit" does not empty his thesis of its import:

> All this "quasi" implies is that this "forma," in spite of its formal causality, which must be taken really seriously, abides in its absolute transcendence (inviolateness, "freedom"). But it does *not* imply that the statement . . . is a mode of speech lacking all binding force; on the

contrary, it is the *quasi* which must be prefixed to every application to God of a category in itself terrestrial.[57]

In Teilhard's case, the "quasi" does not nullify his attribution to Christ of real formal causality; but it does safeguard his thesis from gross pantheism and the crass conception of an (impossible) immediate substantial union between Christ as form and all creatures as matter.

To explicate his fundamental assertion of an intrinsically Christic universe, then, Teilhard recurs to scholastic causal categories. In his very rich but sometimes problematical conception, each causal mode complements the others (efficient, final, and formal), and each illumines another aspect of the universe's intrinsically Christic character. But this is not to say that Teilhard was a skilled scholastic philosopher, or that this causal articulation of his Christic cosmology represents the ultimate expression of his thought. On the contrary, his serious hesitations in this area are well known; he ventures here only in view of the seminary training of his colleagues, hoping by this appeal to categories they will find familiar, to evoke the deeper vision in which he is really interested. The norm of his writings is always experiential rather than speculative; in a characteristic passage, he writes concerning a negative reaction to his essay *The Priest:*

> This friendly criticism has had the salutary effect of making me face the difficulties of practical life, and, incidentally, the slavery imposed on us by a certain group of accepted scholastic formulas (in particular those relating to the various forms of causality). Evidently I must find a certain orthodox way of putting things if I am to get across my "experience" without distorting or *weakening* it. The important thing, fortunately, is that, intrinsically, the experience is orthodox. . . .[58]

This primacy of experience makes Teilhard pass spontaneously from speculative expressions to concrete models:

> Christ is essentially revealed in Scripture as invested with *the power of giving to the World,* in his own person, *its definitive form. . . .* We must ultimately admit that there is *in natura Christi,* some universal *physical reality,* a certain cosmic extension of his Body and Soul.[59]

It is precisely because Christ is human, that he can graft all creation into his glorified Body. Teilhard thus works out a distinctive theological anthropology with a decisively cosmic emphasis, and it is only in light of this anthropology that one can fully appreciate his cosmic Christology. Because his universe is radically evolutionary, moreover, elements are never seen in static juxtaposition; rather, higher forms emerge from and recapitulate lower forms. All elements, but especially man, are profoundly related to the Whole:

> The first thing I saw was that Man alone can help Man to decipher the World. Up to now, Man in his essential characteristics, has been omitted from all scientific theories of Nature.... Either through excessive admiration or lack of esteem, Man is left floating above, or left on the edge of the Universe.... This is the cause of all our present intellectual and moral difficulties. We shall never understand either Man or Nature unless, as the facts demand, we completely replace Man (without destroying him) in the heart of Nature.[60]

Our Christology — theology of the God-*man* — will be falsely constricted, therefore, unless we bear in mind that man himself is indissolubly linked to the whole universe — not merely linked to it, but rooted in it so as to recapitulate it — sum it up.[61] For by the level of his complexity-consciousness, man represents "the axis and leading shoot of evolution,"[62] the "centre of construction of the Universe." [63] Man actualizes his cosmic dimensions as he endeavors to "build the earth":

> This summing up, this welding together of the whole World are not given to us ready-made and complete with the first awakening of consciousness. It is we who, through our own activity, must industriously assemble the widely scattered elements.[64]

Thus "*we hold evolution in our hands,* responsible for its past to its future."[65] "Man bears along with him the world of beings inferior to God."[66]

Just as when Teilhard explains man's rootedness in the universe, so when he discusses man's responsibility for the Whole, Teilhard has recourse to a great variety of models which balance and complement one another. "Building the earth," e.g., should not be taken to imply that the construction remains juxtaposed to the builder. The universe is more accurately seen as *organically converging,* and man is more properly understood as its locus of infolding:

> ... why not assume a Universe that, in one complete all-embracing whole, folds in upon itself until it is interiorized in a growing complexity? ... Man: not simply a zoological type like the others. But man, the nucleus of a movement of infolding and convergence ... on whom and in whom the Universe enfolds itself.[67]

For Teilhard, the traditional image of man the microcosm takes on a new and dynamic character: in the human body is focused and in-folded the entirety of the cosmos.[68]

It may be clearer now why God, to save and fulfill the entire universe, became *man*. Man, rooted in the Whole, sums up, focuses, and recapitulates that Whole. He may not represent the highest form of intelligent life (the angels surpass him), but he does serve as focal point for the convergence of all creation, material and spiritual. Echoing St. Bonaventure and a rich patristic legacy, Teilhard seizes on man's focal position to explain the cosmic dimension of the Incarnation:

> Admist all the centres of consciousness realized or capable of being realized in the World, we represent perhaps the most central. ... Because men occupy this humble [sub-angelic], but *special* place, one sees why the Redeemer of all things, in order to have contact with all things, became incarnate amongst us, in the lowest of the spiritual spheres, precisely "ut repleret omnia."[69]

This richly seminal text suggests that if the chain of being has a hierarchical character (as traditionally assumed) according to the degree of spiritualization of the various levels, still in accord with a more profound norm more importance may devolve upon a lower but centrally situated link (humanity) because it is in that link that the widely variant elements of unity and multiplicity, spirit and matter, are brought together into coincidence.[70] It is from this special center and focus that Christ realizes his plenitude.

The Word assumes a specifically human nature, then, because mankind is the focal point of universal convergence. It must be borne in mind, though, that by humanity Teilhard does not mean merely a multitude of human beings, among which the Second Person assumes one isolated place. Evolution means convergence, totalization, and the key watershed of totalization is precisely at the level of the human. Note the rich organic model Teilhard uses to explain this point:

> Under conditions of distribution which in any other phylum would have led long ago to the break-up into different species, the human verticil as it spreads out remains entire, like a gigantic leaf whose veins, however distinct, remain always joined in a common tissue. With man we find indefinite interfecundation on every level ... the unique spectacle of a "species" capable of achieving something in which all previous species had failed. It has succeeded, not only in becoming cosmopolitan, but in stretching a single organized membrane over the earth without breaking it. ... Really, I can see no coherent, and therefore scientific, way of grouping this immense succession of facts but as a gigantic psycho-biological operation, a sort of *mega-synthesis,* the "super-arrangement" to which all the thinking elements of the earth find themselves today individually and collectively subject.[71]

Thus Teilhard traces the "super-compression upon itself of the noosphere," which in turn produces a "super-organisation, and that again a super-'consciousisation': that, in turn, is followed by a super-super-compression, and so the process continues."[72]

How is this radical totalization of mankind (and, through mankind, of the entire universe) to find its center, ground, and point of convergence? In that prodigious, divine biological operation which is the redeeming Incarnation.[73] Thus mankind, totalizing the universe, becomes itself totalized in the incarnate Christ. This deep union is realized at the spiritual level of love and knowledge, of course, but it must be recognized that there is also a specifically somatic dimension of this universal totalization. Mankind, and supremely the Son of Man, can recapitulate the *entire* creation because in man there is the coincidence of spirit *and matter.*

The ancient Hebrew conception of man mentioned earlier thus finds a resounding echo in Teilhard. Rejecting the then-common view of the body as an isolated fragment of matter separating the human individual from the rest of the cosmos, Teilhard insists that "the Body is the very Universality of things, in as much as they are centred on an animating Spirit. For a soul, to have a body is to be ... rooted in the Cosmos."[74] This cosmic conception of the body, which may at first strike the Hellenized thinker as odd, has gained considerable acceptance recently through the influence of such currents as biblical theology and existential phenomenology.[75]

Teilhard logically insists that the cosmic character of the Incarnation must be considered from this specifically *somatic* point of view: he himself seeks only to proclaim "the innumerable prolongations of [Christ's] incarnate Being in the world of matter . . . the mystery of [Christ's] Flesh, [of Christ] the Soul shining forth through all that surrounds us."[76]

Thus the universal Christification implied in the very mystery of creation itself, is raised to a new level of actualization by the Incarnation, in which Christ "physically" and really unites himself to the entire cosmos. But this union has a specifically somatic character; and since "it is precisely in and through his Body that the Person of the Word unites himself to his creation,"[77] the union is best evoked by the model of the cosmic Body of Christ.

THE UNIVERSE AS REDEEMED IN CHRIST

Our precise concern in this section is, avoiding duplication of existing studies, to discover what light can be shed by Teilhard's soteriology on the intrinsically Christic character of the universe. We can best begin by recalling the organic unity of Teilhard's grasp of the basic Christian mysteries:

> Taken in their full sense, creation, Incarnation, and Redemption are not simply facts localized at a certain point in time and space; they are truly dimensions of the World . . . these historical facts are simply the privileged expression of process having "cosmic" dimensions.[78]

The theme of the redemption of the entire cosmos is, we have said, fundamental for Teilhard, who gives original sin universal scope precisely to vindicate the cosmic scope of the redemption. "The radius of Christ's Lordship and power is 'by definition' the radius of the Redemption," for Christ must emerge as the bond "in quo omnia constant."[79] The Pauline reference comes naturally to Teilhard in this context.

Our question at this point is, what models does Teilhard

use to elucidate this notion of cosmic Redemption? Teilhard comments that soteriology seems to have long been dominated by the model of "expiating reparation," according to which "Christ has been regarded above all as the Lamb burdened with the sins of the world, and the World above all as a fallen mass." But from the very beginning, he argues, the tradition has offered another, radically more positive model for soteriology, that of "reconstruction" or "re-creation." [80] He insists that this latter theme is again gaining pre-eminence because of a variety of influences, including the impact of the new cosmic perspective upon the Christian consciousness. Christian salvation is thus

> primarily, to lead Creation to its fulfillment in divine union; and for this purpose, secondarily, to eliminate the evil forces of regression and dispersion. No longer first to expiate and in addition to restore; but first to create (or "super-create") and for this purpose, in inevitable consequence, to fight against and to compensate for evil.[81]

Teilhard's cosmic perspective thus leads him to transcribe soteriology into a fresh, major key. What must be stressed now is no longer the narrower effect of the blotting out of sin in souls, but rather cosmic super-creation: "Christ can no longer 'justify' man except by that same act super-creating the entire Universe."[82]

Since to create is to unify, and to "super-create" is to unify decisively and establish "fulfillment in divine union," Teilhard must be said to conceive of cosmic Redemption primarily in terms of this model of decisive unification — incorporation into Christ. For Teilhard, "Christ the Redeemer is, as Redeemer, also Christ the Unifier, so much so that it is not from Adam that mankind derives its real unity and solidarity but from Christ."[83] Christ the Redeemer is Christ the principle of unity who binds up the universe and establishes "one flesh":

> The principle of unity who saves a guilty Creation from returning to dust is Christ. By the force of His attraction, by the light of His moral and spiritual teaching, by the binding power of His very existence, Jesus comes to reestablish at the heart of the World the harmony of efforts and the convergence of all things. When we read the Gospel in a straightforward way we see that no idea translates better for our

understanding the *redemptive function of the Word* than the idea of the unification of all flesh in one same Spirit.[84]

"Unification" has a meaning that is, of course, not merely mathematical nor even metaphysical — it is specifically cosmic and Christic, so that it implies *incorporation* into Christ's cosmic Body of the entire course of universal evolution. In returning "to the bosom of the Father" Christ "must creatively carry the noogenesis of the cosmos to the natural term of is maturity."[85]

Teilhard explicates this central redemptive model of cosmic incorporation with a series of subordinate but illustrative models. Redemption is a continual compensation for and correction of the deviations inherent in cosmic evolution.[86] It is a building up, a reconstructing, a recasting of the universe.[87] It means carrying forward toward convergence the evolutionary course of the universe.[88] This latter model finds a particularly fruitful and suggestive application in Teilhard's theology of the Cross. Teilhard wished to move away from the dominant emphasis upon expiation in defeat and solitude for the sins of souls — away from the preoccupation with condemnation of the world. He wished rather to stress the positive and cosmic significance of the Cross:

In its highest and most general sense, the doctrine of the Cross is that to which all men adhere who believe that the vast movement and agitation of human life opens on to a road that leads somewhere, and that that road climbs upward.

Towards the peaks, shrouded in mist from our human eyes, whither the Cross beckons us, we rise by a path which is the way of universal progress. The royal road of the Cross is no more nor less than the road of human endeavor supernaturally righted and prolonged. Once we have fully grasped the meaning of the Cross, we are no longer in danger of finding life sad and ugly. We shall simply have become more attentive to its barely comprehensible solemnity.

To sum up, Jesus on the Cross is both the symbol and the reality of the immense labour of the centuries which has, little by little, raised the created spirit and brought it back to the depths of the Divine Milieu. He represents (and in a true sense, he is) creation, as, upheld by God, it reascends the slopes of being . . . the Cross was placed on the crest of the road which leads to the highest peaks of creation.[89]

Jesus crucified "is not a reject: He is not defeated. On the contrary, He carries the weight of the universal course of progress with Him toward God."[90]

But if Teilhard was able to shape a theology of the Cross with a cosmic and positive cast, it was particularly the mystery of the Resurrection which he felt vindicated the full scope of his vision. "It seemed as if he could not have enough of the Resurrection."[91] Gray directly links Teilhard's concept of Christ's formal causality with his theology of the Resurrection. It is precisely Christ glorified, in his risen Body, who effects in a quasi-formal manner the entire cosmos.[92]

Like the Incarnation itself and the Passion, the Resurrection too becomes cosmic in scope — it becomes the mystery of the decisive centering of the universe on Christ:

> We are often too inclined to regard the Resurrection as an isolated event in time, with an apologetical significance. . . . It is something quite other and much greater than that. It is a "tremendous" [Teilhard uses the English word for emphasis] cosmic event. It marks Christ's effective assumption as the universal Centre. Until that time, he was present in all things as a soul that is painfully gathering together its embryonic elements. Now he radiates over the whole Universe as a consciousness and activity fully in control of themselves. . . . When, presented with a Universe whose physical and spiritual immensity are seen to be ever more bewildering, we are terrified by the constantly increasing weight of energy and glory we have to attribute to the son of Mary if we are to be justified in continuing to worship him, it is then that we should turn our thoughts to the Resurrection.[93]

The key to the cosmic dimensions of Christ and to the Christic character of the universe is thus the mystery of the Resurrection; in its light Teilhard proclaims "the essential function assumed by the risen Christ at the centre and peak of Creation to bring all things to their fulfillment."[94] It is only the risen Christ, pervading all creation and rendering it translucent, that Teilhard can truly worship:

> As long as I could see — or dared see — in you, Lord Jesus, only the man who lived two thousand years ago, the sublime moral teacher, the Friend, the Brother, my love remained timid and constrained. . . . But now, Master, today, when through the manifestation of those superhuman powers with which your Resurrection endowed you, you shine forth from within all the forces of the Earth and so become visible to me, now I recognize you as my Sovereign, and with delight I surrender myself to you.[95]

Through the cosmic import of the Resurrection all creation is rendered potentially instrumental for contact with Christ; the entire universe is rendered an extension of his Body: "By virtue of the Resurrection nothing any longer kills inevitably but everything is capable of becoming the blessed touch of the divine hands, the blessed influence of the will of God upon our lives."[96] In Christ's risen Body the entire universe is transformed. Every created element, and in a particular way every human body, is "rigorously coextensive with the totality of space and time,"[97] but in Christ's case "this coextension of coexistence has become a coextension of domination."[98] And the reason Christ's Body both extends to the totality of creation and dominates the whole universe is to be traced to "the transforming effect of the Resurrection."[99] Thus Teilhard's theology of the intrinsically Christic character of the universe finds its focus once again in the model of the cosmic Body, specifically the cosmic *risen* Body of Christ.

CONCLUSION

Modern man lives with a heightened consciousness of his vast universe, a new awareness of the vital bonds which link him with the whole. This new consciousness poses a challenge to the Christian faith, to think through anew the Christian significance of the universe. It was to this task that Teilhard dedicated his entire life. Such a Christian understanding must somehow link the universe to Christ, God's decisive revelation. Teilhard's central thesis is that the universe is intrinsically and organically Christic, that it constitutes the "cosmic Body of Christ."

Thus the bond between Christ and the universe is not merely extrinsic and juridical; Christ is much more than a real estate owner or manager of creation. At the heart of Teilhard's Christic cosmology is the resolute rejection of such extrinsicism and the vigorous vindication of the universe as cosmic Body of Christ.

An analysis of this model of cosmic Body in the light of the now advanced model methodology indicates that although it must not be taken pictorially (as must not, also, almost all theological, philosophical and scientific models), such a model can be richly evocative and seminal for both Christian theology and spirituality.

Teilhard's vision of the Christic nature of the universe finds powerful expression in his earliest essays. His *Writings in Time of War* already reveal the central crisis of Teilhard's "two loves": his self-donation to God and his total commitment to the universe. And they spell out his resolution of this key crisis through his realization that the universe is intrinsically Christic. Such an intuition does not garb creation in triumphalistic colors, concealing the dimension of conflict and suffering; rather, Teilhard underlines the humble, kenotic quality of Christ's cosmic presence, the torn and imperfect character of a creation still groping toward Omega.

Teilhard's early vision developed and became fully rounded through his contact with the biblical, patristic and theological heritage which affirms the cosmic Christ and the Christic cosmos. This contact was made possible largely through Teilhard's scholarly confreres who encouraged him by noting this wider context of his thought.

Thus the Semitic notion of the body as bond to all creation, the Pauline themes of creation in and through Christ, of the "Pleroma" of Christ — these and similar elements provide the biblical foundation for a Christic theology and spirituality of the universe.

The patristic themes of recapitulation of all things in Christ, of a creation engrafted in the Word Incarnate, etc., advance this Christic conception. Duns Scotus and later Bérulle both vindicate the absolute primary of Christ in the divine intentions, so that Christ is revealed as Exemplar and Prototype, Mediator, Scope and Final Cause of creation. In scholastic theologians such as Peter Galatinus and Ambrogio Catarino Polito, both supporters of the Scotist thesis, one finds these themes focused into the explicit affirmation that all of creation is contained within the glorified Body of Christ.

In our own time Maurice Blondel, also a champion of the Scotist thesis, proposes a "pan-Christism" in which Christ appears as the ground for the organic union of the whole cosmos, as the substantial Bond of all things.

It is in the context of this rich and significant Christian current that Teilhard must be studied. He corresponded and met with Blondel in his formative years; he was quite familiar with the Scotist thesis through Allegra and others; he knew the Christic vision of the Fathers and of Pauline scholarship through such colleagues as de Lubac, de Solages, Huby, and Allegra. And he thought of himself as not merely a private student of this great current, but a member, a spokesman to the modern world of its central Christic vision of creation.

Of course each individual thinker in this Christian current brought his own unique emphasis, language, and conceptual framework to the interpretation of the Christian mystery. Teilhard's distinctive contributions to this heritage certainly include his post-Darwinian evolutionary perspective of the universe, his affirmation that cosmogenesis is convergent and culminates in "Christogenesis," and similar original insights. Also, Teilhard emphasizes in a particularly explicit way the significance of "building the earth," of developing man's world for the true progress of the human spirit.

Teilhard's concrete and vivid model of "cosmic Body of Christ" finds its speculative complement in his interrelated concepts of the universe as organic unity and as intrinsically Christic.

Teilhard argues, on the basis of intuition, but also of scientific presupposition and verification, that the universe is not a mere collection of juxtaposed fragments but rather a totum, an organic *whole*. Moreover, this whole is a *dynamic* coherence in which every element is intrinsically related to every other in cosmic evolution. Man represents the highest shoot of the upper thrust of this evolution; as microcosm, moreover, man focuses and totalizes this whole. And since in the Incarnation it is precisely human nature that is assumed by the Word, Christ can thus effect the ultimate totalization and recapitulation of the universe in the mysteries of creation, Incarnation, and Redemption.

Regarding creation, it is not that Christ comes to a pre-established universe and merely claims juridical title to it as its lord; rather (as the Scotistic heritage insists), the very shaping, the primordial forming of creation occurs *in Christ;* thus, as Teilhard goes on to insist, Christ exercises upon the whole of creation a quasi-formal causality.

The Incarnation establishes Christ physically at the heart of the cosmos; it thus initiates the mystery of Redemption. The Incarnation is consequently conceived in cosmic and organic terms, as an actual "taking root" in the whole, an assimilation of the whole.

The Redemption in its full extension again reveals the cosmic dimension of Christ's action. Thus what is at issue in Christ's salvific work is not merely an expiation for the individual sins of the faithful; rather, Redemption signifies as well the "super-creation" of the universe. Teilhard spells out this cosmic scope of soteriology in terms of the models of organic unification, of incorporation into the cosmic Body of

Christ. The universe receives its new life by being engrafted into the cosmic, resurrected Body of Christ.

Thus the central Christian mysteries of creation, Incarnation and Redemption are seen by Teilhard as advancing phases of one divine creative-salvific action. This action brings to ever higher realization the intrinsically Christic character of the universe.

The model of cosmic Body (and a cluster of related models) accompanies this theology, nourishing and illustrating its statement that all of creation is to be seen as inserted in the full mystery of Christ.

LIST OF ESSAYS BY TEILHARD
CITED IN THIS VOLUME

The following alphabetical list of essays is supplied to facilitate location of full bibliographical data for these essays, which were cited as economically as possible in the footnotes. For each title, there are furnished below the *English* volume of Teilhard's works, and the pages within that volume where the English version of the essay can be found. Here too, in the interests of economy, abbreviations have been used to indicate the English volumes; a key is found immediately following the list. Finally, in those few cases where a French essay has not yet been translated, the French source is furnished; and, of course, unpublished essays are so indicated.

"Agitation ou Genèse"	FM 222-35.
"L'Ame du monde"	WTW 177-90.
"La Centrologie"	AE 97-127.
"Ce que le monde attend en ce moment de l'église de Dieu"	CE 212-20.
"Le Christ dans la matière"	HU 41-55.
"Le Christ Evoluteur"	CE 138-50.
"Le Christianisme dans le monde"	SC 98-112.
"Le Christique"	unpublished.
"Christologie et évolution"	CE 76-95.
"Chute, Rédemption et Géocentrie"	CE 36-44.
"Le Coeur de la matière"	unpublished.
"Comment je crois"	CE 96-132.
"Comment je vois"	unpublished.
"Le Dieu de l'évolution"	CE 237-43.
"L'Elément universel"	WTW 289-302.
"L'Energie humaine"	HE 19-47.
"En quoi consiste le corps humain?"	SC 11-13.
"L'Esprit de la terre"	HE 19-47.
"Esquisse d'une dialectique de l'esprit"	AE 141-51.
"Forma Christi"	WTW 249-69.
"La Grande option"	FM 36-63.
"L'Histoire naturelle du monde"	VP 103-13.
"Introduction à la vie chrétienne"	CE 151-72.
"La Lutte contre la multitude"	WTW 93-114.
"La Messe sur le monde"	HU 19-37.
"Le Milieu mystique"	WTW 115-49.
"Mon Univers" (1918)	untranslated – ET 263-79.
"Mon Univers" (1924)	SC 37-85.

"La Mystique de la science"	HE 163-81.
"Note pour servir à l'évangelisa- tion des temps nouveaux"	untranslated — ET 363-81.
"Note sur le Christ universel"	SC 14-20.
"Note sur les modes de l'action divine dans l'Univers"	CE 25-35.
"Le Paradoxe transformiste"	VP 80-102.
"Le Prêtre"	WTW 203-24.
"La Puissance spirituelle de la Matière"	HU 59-71.
"Que faut-il penser du transfor- misme?"	VP 151-60.
"Quelques vues générales sur l'es- sence du Christianisme"	CE 133-37.
"Réflexions sur la conversion du monde"	SC 118-27.
"Réflexions sur le péché originel"	CE 187-98.
"Science et Christ"	SC 21-36.
"Un Seuil mental sous nos pas: Du Cosmos à la Cosmogénèse	AE 251-68.
"La Signification et la valeur constructrice de la souffrance"	HE 48-52.
"Super-humanité — Super-Christ — Super-Charité"	SC 151-73.
"Sur la notion de transformation créatrice"	CE 21-24.
"Sur la valeur religieuse de la recherche"	SC 199-205.
"L'Union créatrice"	WTW 151-76.
"Universalisation et union"	AE 77-95.
"La Vie cosmique"	WTW 13-71.
"Vie et planètes"	FM 101-28.

KEY TO ABBREVIATIONS USED ABOVE

AE   — *Activation of Energy* (New York: Harcourt Brace Jovanovich, 1971).

CE   — *Christianity and Evolution* (New York: Harcourt Brace Jovanovich, 1971).

FM   — *The Future of Man* (New York: Harper & Row, 1964).

HE   — *Human Energy* (London: Collins, 1969).

HU   — *Hymn of the Universe* (New York: Harper & Row, 1965).

SC   — *Science and Christ* (New York: Harper & Row, 1968).

VP   — *The Vision of the Past* (New York: Harper & Row, 1966).

WTW — *Writings in Time of War* (New York: Harper & Row, 1967).
       [ET refers to the French edition, which contains seven essays not found in the English translation: *Ecrits du temps de la guerre* (1916–1919) (Paris: Grasset, 1965).]

Footnotes

PREFACE

1. Teilhard, "Super-humanité – Super-Christ – Super-charité" (1943), English trans. in *Science and Christ* (New York: Harper & Row, 1968), p. 151.

2. Cf. Robert Jastrow, *Red Giants and White Dwarfs: Man's Descent from the Stars* (New York: New American Library, Signet Books, 1969), pp. 11–36.

3. Cf. Lincoln Barnett, *The Universe and Dr. Einstein* (New York: Grosset & Dunlap, Bantam Books, 1968), p. 93.

4. *Ibid.,* p. 113.   5. Cited *ibid.,* p. 108.

6. Robert T. Francoeur, *Evolving World, Converging Man* (New York: Holt, Rinehart & Winston, 1970), p. 59.

7. Teilhard, "Christologie et évolution" (1933), English trans. in *Christianity and Evolution* (New York: Harcourt Brace Jovanovich, 1971), pp. 91–92.

8. Teilhard, letter of 12/13/18, English trans. in *The Making of a Mind* (New York: Harper & Row, 1965), pp. 267–68.

9. Robert Butterworth, S. J., *The Theology of Creation* (Notre Dame, Ind.: Fides Publishers, 1969), p. 89.

10. Teilhard, "Comment je crois" (1934), English trans. in *Christianity and Evolution,* p. 128.

11. Butterworth, p. 23.

12. Cf. N. M. Wildiers, O.F.M.Cap., *An Introduction to Teilhard de Chardin,* trans. Hubert Hoskins (New York: Harper & Row, 1968), p. 47.

13. There is no area of theology unaffected by this vision, but one thinks immediately of the theology of grace, spiritual theology, sacramentology, ecclesiology, and eschatology.

CHAPTER ONE

1. Cf. Henri de Lubac, S. J., *The Religion of Teilhard de Chardin,* trans. René Hague (New York: Desclée, 1967), pp. 189–94.

2. Thus argue some theologians of the Roman school; cf. e.g., Philippe de

la Trinité, O.C.D., *Rome et Teilhard de Chardin* (Paris: Librairie Arthème Fayard, 1964), pp. 172, 177.

3. Pope Pius XII, *Mystici Corporis* (Washington: NCWC, 1943), pp. 3, 7.

4. Ian T. Ramsey, *Religious Language: An Empirical Placing of Theological Phrases* (New York: Macmillan, 1963), p. 56.

5. Ewert Cousins, "Models and the Future of Theology," *Continuum* 7 (1969), pp. 80-82.

6. *Ibid.,* p. 82.

7. Teilhard, "Le Dieu d'évolution" (1953), English trans. in *Christianity and Evolution,* p. 240.

8. Teilhard, "Note sur les modes de l'action divine dans l'Univers" (1920), Eng. trans., *ibid.,* p. 25.

9. Teilhard, "L'énergie humaine" (1937), English trans. in *Human Energy* (London: Collins, 1969), p. 155.

10. de Lubac, p. 18.

11. Christopher F. Mooney, S. J., *Teilhard de Chardin and the Mystery of Christ* (New York: Harper & Row, 1966), p. 211.

12. Cf. Cousins, pp. 86-87: "Perhaps the most striking example of the cosmic sense in contemporary theology is in the thought of Teilhard de Chardin. His profound cosmic sense converged with his scientific knowledge and Christian faith to produce an evolutionary vision and a cosmic theology."

13. John McIntyre, *The Shape of Christology* (Philadelphia: Westminster Press, 1966), p. 64.

14. Ramsey, p. 81.   15. *Ibid.,* p. 69.

16. Jörg Splett, "Body," in *Sacramentum Mundi: An Encyclopedia of Theology,* ed. Karl Rahner *et al.* (New York: Herder & Herder, 1968), 1:233.

17. *Ibid.*   18. *Ibid.*

19. Teilhard, "En quoi consiste le corps humain?" (1919), Eng. trans. in *Science and Christ,* p. 13. One finds this same stress on the mysteriously cosmic dimension of the human body in many currents of contemporary theology. Cf. Karl Rahner, S. J., *On the Theology of Death,* vol. 2 of *Quaestiones Disputatae* (New York: Herder & Herder, 1967), pp. 18-19. It is also a prominent theme in comparative religions—cf. R. C. Zaehner, "Teilhard and Eastern Religions," *The Teilhard Review* 2 (Winter 1967/8), p. 51—of psychology—cf., Carl G. Jung *et al., Man and His Symbols* (New York: Doubleday, 1970), p. 200; and even of psychedelic experience—cf. R. E. L. Masters and Jean Houston, *The Varieties of Psychedelic Experience* (New York: Holt, Rinehart & Winston, 1966), pp. 67 ff.

20. McIntyre, p. 58.

21. Sometimes models and their qualifiers do seem to be held together only through the force exerted upon them by their conceivers. This writer remembers a spiritual conference offered in Rome on the topic of Mary as the "spiritual Maginot line of the Italian people."

22. Ian T. Ramsey, *Christian Discourse* (London: Oxford University Press, 1965), p. 20.

23. McIntyre, p. 80.   24. Ramsey, *Christian Discourse*, p. 20.

25. Mooney, p. 170.

26. Teilhard, "La Messe sur le monde" (1923), Eng. trans. in *Hymn of the Universe* (New York: Harper & Row, 1965), pp. 36–37.

27. Madeleine Barthélemy-Madaule, *La Personne et le drame humain chez Teilhard de Chardin* (Paris: Éditions du Seuil, 1967), p. 268.

28. McIntyre, p. 73.

29. James Michael Connolly, "The Heavenly Priesthood of Jesus as the Model for the Theology of Liturgy" (Ph.D. thesis, Department of Theology, Fordham University, 1967), pp. 17–18.

30. McIntyre, p. 75.   31. Cf. Chapter IV, below.

32. Ian T. Ramsey, *Models and Mystery* (London: Oxford University Press, 1964), pp. 16–17.

33. McIntyre, p. 80.

34. One should note the importance in Teilhard's writings of such terms as "action," "activance," "activation," "activités," "co-conscientisation," "cohérence," "co-réflexion," "création," etc. See Claude Cuénot, *Nouveau Lexique Teilhard de Chardin* (Paris: Éditions du Seuil, 1968), *passim*.

35.Teilhard, *The Divine Milieu*, trans. Bernard Wall (New York: Harper & Row, 1965), pp. 49–73.

36. *Ibid.*, p. 137.

37. Teilhard, "Le Coeur de la Matière" (1950), unpublished, p. 25.

38. McIntyre, p. 63; cf. also p. 65.

39. Ramsey, *Models and Mystery*, p. 48; cf. McIntyre, p. 61.

40. Teilhard, "La Vie cosmique" (1916), Eng. trans. in *Writings in Time of War* (New York: Harper & Row, 1967), pp. 49–50.

41. John A. T. Robinson, *The Body: A Study in Pauline Theology* (London: SCM Press, 1963), p. 51.

42. McIntyre, pp. 68–69.

43. Cf. Ramsey, *Models and Mystery*, pp. 60–61.

44. Cf., e.g., Teilhard, "La Vie cosmique," *loc. cit.* (note 40, above).

45. Cf. Mooney, pp. 13 ff., and Robert Speaight, *The Life of Teilhard de Chardin* (New York: Harper & Row, 1967), pp. 24 ff.

46. Cf. Mooney, pp. 104 ff.

47. Cf. Karl Rahner and Herbert Vorgrimler, *Theological Dictionary*, trans. Richard Strachan (New York: Herder & Herder, 1965), p. 408: "According to St. Paul the Christian's risen body is 'spiritual' . . . conformed to Christ's glorious body . . . but, analogous to the Lord's glorified body, preserving continuity with the earthly body, though changed (1 Cor. 15:36 f; 51)."

48. Ramsey, *Models and Mystery*, p. 60.

49. Rudolph Schnackenburg and Jacques Dupont, O.S.B., "The Church as the People of God," in *Concilium*, vol. 1: *The Church and Mankind* (Glen Rock, N.J.: Paulist Press, 1964), p. 119.

50. Boniface Willems, O. P., "Who Belongs to the Church?" *Ibid.*, p. 136.

51. Ramsey, *Models and Mystery*, p. 61.

52. Ramsey, *Religious Language,* p. 41.

53. Teilhard, "Le Prêtre" (1918), Eng. trans. in *Writings in Time of War,* p. 208.

54. Cf. John Macquarrie, *Twentieth Century Religious Thought* (New York: Harper & Row, 1963), p. 317.

55. Teilhard, "Le Coeur de la Matière," p. 1.

56. Cf. Mooney, p. 211, and de Lubac, p. 19.

57. Petro Bilaniuk, "The Christology of Teilhard de Chardin," in *Proceedings of the Teilhard Conference 1964* (New York: Fordham University, 1964), p. 112.

58. Zaehner, p. 42: cf. "Teilhard Mystique," in Claude Cuénot, "Science et Foi chez Teilhard de Chardin," *Études Teilhardiennes* 1 (1968), pp. 5–10.

59. Christian d'Armagnac, "Le Premier Teilhard: Le Christ et le Monde," *Études* 109 (mai 1965), p. 654.

60. Teilhard, letter of 3/31/17, Eng. trans. in *The Making of a Mind,* p. 192.

61. Teilhard, "Sur la valeur religieuse de la Recherche" (1947). Eng. trans. in *Science and Christ,* p. 203.

62. Teilhard, "Mon Univers" (1918), *Écrits du temps de la guerre, 1916–1919* (Paris: Grasset, 1965), p. 272; the essay is not translated in *Writings in Time of War.*

63. Teilhard, "Le Coeur de la Matière," p. 2.

64. *Ibid.,* pp. 3–4.   65. Mooney, p. 22.

66. Teilhard, "Le Coeur de la Matière," p. 20.

67. Speaight, p. 31; cf. Cuénot, "Science et Foi . . . ," p. 7.

68. Teilhard, "Le Christianisme dans le Monde" (1933), Eng. trans. in *Science and Christ,* p. 107. On Teilhard's "passionate taste for the World," see his letter of 9/23/34 in *Letters from a Traveller* (New York: Harper & Row, 1962), p. 206.

69. Teilhard, "Science et Christ" (1921), trans. *ibid.,* pp. 61–62.

70. *Ibid.*

71. Karl Rahner, S. J., *Nature and Grace,* trans. Dinah Wharton (New York: Sheed & Ward, 1964), pp. 115, 118.

72. Teilhard, "Le Christianisme dans le Monde," p. 103.

73. Teilhard, "La Puissance spirituelle de la Matière" (1919), Eng. trans. in *Hymn of the Universe,* p. 65.

74. Mircea Eliade, *Myths, Dreams and Mysteries,* trans. Philip Mairet (New York: Harper & Row, 1957), p. 155.

75. Teilhard, *The Divine Milieu,* pp. 59–60.   76. *Ibid.,* pp. 107–11.

77. Cf. Anselmo Stolz, O.S.B., *Teologia della Mistica,* trans. Martino Matronola, O.S.B. (Brescia: Morcelliana, 1940), pp. 105–28: "La scala del paradiso." On the sacramentality of the universe, Cipriano Vagaggini, O.S.B., *Il Senso Teologico della Liturgia* (Roma: Edizioni Paoline, 1965), pp. 611 ff. For the empirical approach, William James, *Varieties of Religious Experience* (New York: Longmans, Green, 1919), p. 41. And for the theological, W. R. Inge, *Christian Mysticism* (New York: Meridian Books, 1956), p. 299.

78. Cf., e.g., Mooney, pp. 179 ff.

79. Bilaniuk, p. 112.

80. Claude Cuénot, *Teilhard de Chardin: A Biographical Study,* trans. Vincent Colimore (Baltimore: Helicon, 1965), pp. 376–77.

81. Teilhard, "Réflexions sur la Conversion du Monde" (1936), Eng. trans. in *Science and Christ,* p. 124.

82. Teilhard, "Le Christique" (1955), unpublished, p. 2.

CHAPTER TWO

1. Cf. André Monestier, *Pour Teilhard de Chardin* (Nancy: Berger-Levrault, 1967), pp. 8–9.

2. Teilhard, letter of 4/9/16; Eng. trans. in *The Making of a Mind,* p. 99.

3. Teilhard, "La Vie cosmique," p. 14.

4. Here recall Ramsey's analysis of religious language as arising from a discernment situation and ordered toward evoking disclosure and commitment. Cf. Ian T. Ramsey, *Religious Language,* pp. 19 ff.

5. Teilhard, "La Vie cosmique," pp. 49–50.　　6. *Ibid.,* pp. 57–58.

7. Teilhard, "Mon Univers" (1918), p. 271.　　8. *Ibid.,* pp. 272–73.

9. Teilhard, "La Vie cosmique," p. 59.　　10. *Ibid.*

11. Teilhard, letter of 1/9/17; *The Making of a Mind,* p. 130.

12. Cuénot, *Teilhard . . .* , p. 40; cf. Speaight, pp. 49–81.

13. Teilhard, "Le Christ dans la Matière" (1916); Eng. trans. in *Hymn of the Universe,* pp. 42–55.

14. *Ibid.,* pp. 42–43.　　15. *Ibid.,* p. 48.

16. Cf. e.g., Wildiers in his introduction to *Hymn of the Universe,* pp. 13–15.

17. Philippe de la Trinité, *Rome et Teilhard de Chardin,* p. 129.

18. Teilhard, "Le Milieu mystique" (1917), Eng. trans. in *Writings in Time of War,* p. 146.

19. For a recent discussion of this subject see A. Poulain, S.J., *The Graces of Interior Prayer,* trans. Leonora Smith (London: Routledge & Kegan Paul, 1949), pp. 88 ff.

20. Teilhard, "Le Milieu mystique," p. 146.

21. Teilhard, "L'Union créatrice" (1917); Eng. trans. in *Writings in Time of War,* p. 174.

22. Donald P. Gray, *The One and the Many: Teilhard de Chardin's Vision of Unity* (New York: Herder & Herder, 1969), p. 32.

23. Teilhard, "L'Union créatrice," p. 174.

24. Cf. Cuénot, *Lexique. . .* , p. 58.

25. Teilhard, "Mon Univers" (1918), p. 272.　　26. *Ibid.,* p. 278.

27. Teilhard, "Le Prêtre," p. 205.　　28. *Ibid.,* p. 208.

29. *Ibid.,* p. 210.　　30. *Ibid.,* p. 218.

31. Teilhard, "Forma Christi" (1918); Eng. trans. in *Writings in Time of War,* p. 250.

32. *Ibid.*, pp. 267-68.

33. Teilhard, "Note pour servir à l'évangelisation des temps nouveaux" (1919), *Écrits du temps de la guerre*, p. 369 (the essay is not translated).

34. *Ibid.*, pp. 374-75.

35. Teilhard, letter of 2/19/19; Eng. trans. in *The Making of a Mind*, p. 373.

36. Teilhard, "L'Élément universel" (1919); Eng. trans. in *Writings in Time of War*, pp. 290-91.

37. *Ibid.*, p. 296.

38. Cf. R. Garrigou-Lagrange, O.P., *Christian Perfection and Contemplation*, trans. Sister M. Timothea Doyle (London: Herder, 1937), pp. 337-71.

39. St. Teresa alerts mystics to this temptation repeatedly; see *The Complete Works of St. Teresa of Jesus*, trans. E. Allison Peers (London: Sheed & Ward, 1946), 1:55, 71, 79; 2:106, 305 ff., etc.

40. Teilhard, letter of 8/2/19; Eng. trans. in *The Making of a Mind*, p. 298.

41. *Ibid.*

42. Teilhard, "La Puissance spirituelle de la Matière," p. 60.

43. *Ibid.*, p. 64.   44. *Ibid.*, p. 67.   45. *Ibid.*, p. 69.

CHAPTER THREE

1. Teilhard, "Agitation ou Genèse" (1947), Eng. trans. in *The Future of Man* (New York: Harper & Row, 1964), p. 224.

2. Cf., e.g., Gabriel M. Allegra, O.F.M., *My Conversations with Teilhard de Chardin on the Primacy of Christ*, trans. Bernardino M. Bonansea, O.F.M. (Chicago: Franciscan Herald Press, 1970), p. 41.

3. Cf. *ibid.*, p. 26; and Speaight, pp. 327-28.

4. Henri de Lubac, S.J., *Teilhard Explained* (Glen Rock, N.J.: Paulist Deus Books, 1966), p. 14.

5. Teilhard, "Mon Univers" (1924), Eng. trans. in *Science and Christ*, p. 54.

6. de Lubac, *Teilhard Explained*, p. 14.

7. Allegra notes (p. 27) that Teilhard "drew heavily from the teaching of St. Paul, whom he used to read in the original Greek."

8. See the pregnant exposition of Robinson (*op. cit.*, p. 48).

9. *Ibid.*, p. 21.

10. F. X. Durrwell, C.Ss.R., *The Resurrection: A Biblical Study*, trans. Rosemary Sheed (New York: Sheed & Ward, 1960), pp. 115-16.

11. Joseph Huby, S.J., *Saint Paul: Les Epîtres de la Captivité* (Paris: Beauchesne, 1947), p. 40.

12. Robert L. Faricy, S.J., "Individual, Societal, and Cosmic Dimensions of Salvation," *Theological Studies* 30 (1969), p. 468.

13. Stanislas Lyonnet, S.J., "The Redemption of the Universe," *Contem-*

porary New Testament Studies, ed. Sister M. Rosalie Ryan, C.S.J. (College-ville, Minn.: Liturgical Press, 1965), pp. 425-28.

14. *Ibid.,* p. 428.   15. Huby, p. 46.   16. Lyonnet, p. 434.

17. Allegra, p. 66.   18. Col. 1:20; cf. Rom 8:21.

19. Cf. Huby, pp. 45 ff.   20. *Ibid.*   21. Durrwell, p. 116.

22. Mooney, p. 97.   23. Allegra, pp. 65, 67.   24. Eph. 1:10.

25. Lyonnet, p. 432; cf. Rudolph Schnackenburg, *The Church in the New Testatment,* trans. W. J. O'Hara (New York: Herder & Herder, 1966), pp. 185-87; and Lucien Cerfaux, *La Theologie de l'Église suivant s. Paul* (Paris: Éditions du Cerf, 1947), pp. 257-58.

26. Thus the *Jerusalem Bible;* also Mooney, p. 98.

27. Cf. e.g., Schnackenburg, p. 185.   28. Mooney, p. 97.

29. Ernest Best, *One Body in Christ: A Study of the Relationship of the Church to Christ in the Epistles of the Apostle Paul* (London: S.P.C.K., 1955), p. 123.

30. Schnackenburg, p. 185.   31. Faricy, p. 468.

32. Martin Dibelius, *An die Kolosser Epheser an Philemon* (Tübingen: J.C.B. Mohr, 1953), pp. 36-37; Heinrich Schlier, *Der Brief au die Epheser* (Dusseldorf: Patmos-Verlag, 1958), pp. 207-09.

33. Schlier points out, though, that Paul's concept differs from that of Greco-Roman culture particularly in that for Paul "body" and "head" denote precisely one "man."

34. Émile Rideau, *The Thought of Teilhard de Chardin,* trans. René Hague (New York: Harper & Row, 1967).

35. Mooney, p. 96.

36. Cf. Bruno de Solages, *Teilhard de Chardin* (Toulouse: Privat, 1967), pp. 355-56; de Lubac, *Teilhard Explained,* pp. 15-17; and Wildiers, p. 140.

37. Teilhard, "La Vie cosmique," pp. 49-50.

38. See Henri de Lubac, S.J., *Teilhard de Chardin: The Man and His Meaning,* trans. René Hague (New York: Hawthorn, 1965), pp. 49-52.

39. De Lubac remarks (*ibid.,* p. 49) that Teilhard refers to the Fathers "in general and rather inexact ways."

40. Mooney, p. 233, n. 44; cf. Rideau, p. 528, n. 82.

41. De Lubac, Teilhard's close friend with whom he was frequently in contact, acknowledges his own debt to Mersch; see his *Catholicism: A Sudy of Dogma in Relation to the Corporate Destiny of Mankind,* trans. Lancelot C. Sheppard (New York: Sheed & Ward, 1958), xiv, n. 6.

42. Émile Mersch, *Le Corps mystique du Christ* (Paris, 1936), p. 226.

43. F. L. Cross, *The Early Christian Fathers* (London: Duckworth, 1960), pp. 109-15.

44. Cf. de Lubac, *Teilhard de Chardin . . . ,* p. 49; Rideau, pp. 532-33, n. 90; Allegra, p. 42. Huby and de Lubac have engaged in special study of Ireneaus.

45. Teilhard, "La Mystique de la science" (1939); Eng. trans. in *Human Energy* (London: Collins, 1969), p. 167, n. 1.

46. George A. Maloney, S.J., *The Cosmic Christ: From Paul to Teilhard* (New York: Sheed & Ward, 1968), p. 108.

47. Albert Houssiau, *La Christologie de saint Irénée* (Louvain: Publications Universitaires de Louvain, 1955), p. 216; Maloney, p. 295, n. 9; Mersch, p. 230.

48. Mersch, p. 220.   49. Irenaeus, *Adversus Haereses*, V, 21, 1.

50. Maloney, pp. 109–10; cf. Mersch, p. 230.   51. Maloney, p. 112.

52. Cross, p. 122.   53. Maloney, p. 120.

54. Origen, *On First Principles*, II, 1, 3; cf. Plato, *Timaeus*, 30AB.

55. *Ibid.*, II, 11, 6; cf. IV, 4, 2.

56. Origen, *Homily II on Psalm 36* (*P.G.*, 12:1330 AB). De Lubac cites this text in support of Teilhard —cf. *Teilhard de Chardin* . . . , p. 50.

57. Athanasius, *Oratio de Incarnatione Verbi*, 41 (*P.G.*, 25:168B).

58. Mersch, pp. 264–65.

59. Athanasius, *Ad Serapionem*, I, 25 (*P.G.*, 26:589B).

60. Cf. Teilhard, "Mon Univers" (1924), p. 76.

61. Gregory of Nyssa, *In Illud: Tunc ipse filius subjicietur* (*P.G.*, 40:1317C); cf. Mersch, p. 319.

62. Maloney, p. 166.

63. Cyril of Alexandria, *In Johannem*, 11:11 (*P.G.* 74:557C).

64. Mersch, p. 345.   65. de Lubac, *Teilhard de Chardin* . . . , p. 49.

66. Mersch, p. 453.   67. *Ibid.*, p. 492.

68. Mooney, p. 200; de Lubac, *Teilhard de Chardin* . . . , pp. 142–43, 157; Speaight, pp. 107–08.

69. St. Thomas Aquinas, *Summa Contra Gentiles*, IV, 97.

70. Only once, in "Esquisse d'une dialectique de l'esprit" (1946); Eng. trans. in *Activation of Energy* (New York: Harcourt Brace Jovanovich, 1971), p. 158.

71. Allegra, pp. 92, 95. Cf. p. 107, where Teilhard is quoted as calling the Scotist synthesis "all well-knit and firm," and pp. 95, 104, and 107, where he warmly urges Allegra to bend every effort to propagate it.

72. *Ibid.*, pp. 90–91.

73. Dominic J. Unger, O.F.M.Cap., "Franciscan Christology: Absolute and Universal Primacy of Christ," *Franciscan Studies* 2 (1942), p. 430.

74. Allan B. Wolter, O.F.M., "Duns Scotus on the Predestination of Christ," *The Cord* 5 (1955), p. 367.

75. Wildiers, p. 132.

76. Cf. A. Kleinhans, "De Vita et Operibus Petri Galatini," *Antonianum* 1 (1926), pp. 145–79.

77. Mersch, p. 492.   78. *Ibid.*

79. Cf. Diomede Scaramuzzi, O.F.M., "Le idee scotiste di un grande teologo domenicano," *Collectanea Franciscana* 6 (1963), pp. 197–217.

80. Mersch, pp. 492–93.

81. Cf. Paul Cochois, *Bérulle et l'École française* (Paris: Éditions du Seuil, 1963), p. 166.

82. Allegra, p. 46.   83. de Lubac, *Teilhard de Chardin* . . . , p. 52.

84. R. Bellemare, *Le Sens de la créature dans la doctrine Bérulle* (Paris: Desclée, 1959), pp. 140–42; cf. pp. 128 and 163.

85. For Bérulle's citation of the Fathers, see, e.g., his *Oeuvres complètes*

(Paris: Migne, 1856), cols. 335, 657, 715, etc. On the Greek Fathers, see Mersch, p. 553.

86. Bellemare, p. 124.

87. Michel Dupuy, *Bérulle: Une spiritualité de l'adoration* (Paris: Desclée, 1964), p. 193.

88. *Ibid.,* p. 65.   89. Bérulle, col. 1154.   90. Bellemare, p. 127.

91. Cochois, p. 80. Dupuy (p. 185) argues that Bérulle's development was more gradual.

92. Bérulle, cols. 160 ff.   93. Cochois, p. 83.

94. Cited in Bellemare, pp. 139–40, n. 47.   95. Bérulle, cols. 166–67.

96. *Ibid.,* col. 515; cf. cols. 539, 914.   97. *Ibid.,* col. 184.

98. Bérulle, cited in Cochois, p. 79.   99. Bérulle, col. 745.

100. de Lubac, *Teilhard de Chardin . . .* , p. 52; for the entire text, cf. Bérulle, cols. 398–99.

101. Cf. Rideau, p. 375.

102. See de Lubac's Preface to Pierre Teilhard de Chardin and Maurice Blondel, *Correspondence,* trans. William Whitman (New York: Herder & Herder, 1967), *passim;* cf. Rideau, p. 109.

103. Teilhard, letter of 2/15/55, cited in Cuénot, *Teilhard de Chardin,* p. 39.

104. Mooney, p. 220, n. 26. For Teilhard's influence on Blondel, see Teilhard and Blondel, *Correspondence,* pp. 13, 20, 21.

105. Speaight, p. 105.

106. Cf. John J. McNeil, S.J., *The Blondelian Synthesis: A Study of the Influence of German Philosophical Sources on the Formation of Blondel's Method and Thought* (Leiden: Brill, 1966), p. 294.

107. Teilhard and Blondel, *Correspondence,* p. 26.   108. *Ibid.,* p. 24.

109. See the encyclicals of Leo XIII, *Inscrutabili Dei Consilio* (1878), and *Aeterni Patris* (1879), and his Briefs relating to the foundation of the Roman Academy of St. Thomas (1879) and of the Institut Supérieur de Philosophie at Louvain (1894). Yves Congar recalls that he "was brought up with a kind of contempt for all moderns. Everyone who had written after St. Thomas was rejected"—cited in Patrick Granfield, O.S.B., "Interview with Yves Congar," *America* 116 (5/6/67), p. 676.

110. Maurice Blondel, *The Letter on Apologetics and History and Dogma,* trans. Alexander Dru and Illtyd Trethowan (New York: Holt, Rinehart & Winston, 1964), pp. 201–02.

111. Jean Lacroix, *Maurice Blondel,* trans. John C. Guinness (New York: Sheed & Ward, 1963), pp. 22–23.

112. Teilhard and Blondel, *Correspondence,* p. 22.

113. Blondel, *Journal,* 14 mars, 1890. Both these passages parallel Teilhard's views very closely.

114. Henri Bouillard, *Blondel et le Christianisme* (Paris: Éditions du Seuil, 1961), p. 160.

115. Teilhard and Blondel, *Correspondence,* p. 23.

116. Blondel, *Letter on Apologetics,* pp. 202–03. The Christology gets tied to an epistemological problematic heavily influenced by German philoso-

phy, so that it is no longer simply identifiable with the Scotist position. Throughout his career, Blondel seems to have entertained a "rather baffling notion of Christ's mediation as the final explanation of objective knowledge" — Trethowan, *ibid.*, p. 202, n. 1.

117. Maurice Blondel and Auguste Valensin, *Correspondance 1899-1912* (Paris: Aubier, 1957), 1:49.

118. Teilhard and Blondel, *Correspondence*, p. 21.

119. Blondel and Valensin, 1:44; but cf. the Teilhard-Blondel *Correspondence,* pp. 66-67, n. 12, for the difference of emphasis between Blondel and Teilhard; and *ibid.*, pp. 58-59, n. 1, on the more cautious position later adopted by Blondel.

120. Editor's Note in Blondel and Valensin, 1:43.

121. Teilhard and Blondel, *Correspondence,* p. 23.

122. Blondel, *Une énigme historique: le 'Vinculum Substantiale' d'après Leibnitz et l'ébauche d'une réalisme supérieur* (Paris: Beauchesne, 1930).

123. Mersch, pp. 497-98.

124. Such criticisms as Maritain's, then, that there is "nothing Christian but the name" in Teilhard's use of categories like creation, spirit, evil, God, and the cross, are gratuitous and groundless. See Jacques Maritain, *The Peasant of the Garonne,* trans. Michael Cuddihy (New York: Holt, Rinehart & Winston, 1968), pp. 267-68 and *passim.*

CHAPTER FOUR

1. Teilhard, *The Phenomenon of Man,* trans. Bernard Wall (New York: Harper & Row Torchbooks, new ed., 1965), pp. 41, 43, 44, 215.

2. Cf., e.g., Teilhard, "Le Prêtre," p. 212.

3. Robert Coffy, *Teilhard de Chardin et le socialisme* (Lyon: Chronique sociale de France, 1966), p. 21.

4. Gray, p. 156.

5. As Coffy observes (p. 21) in this context, "one searches always for that which, more or less, one has already discovered."

6. Wildiers, p. 105.   7. Teilhard, "Comment je crois," p. 101.

8. *Ibid.*   9. Teilhard, *The Phenomenon of Man,* p. 31.

10. Teilhard, "Comment je crois," pp. 101-02.   11. *Ibid.*

12. On the delicate theological points this affirmation raises, cf. Mooney, pp. 206-09; and de Lubac, *The Religion of Teilhard de Chardin,* trans. René Hague (New York: Desclée, 1967), pp. 175-76, and *Teilhard de Chardin. . .*, pp. 166 ff.

13. Teilhard often uses "sense" with the connotation of "intuition"; cf. Rideau, p. 440, n. 45. Note also the parallel with Jung on psychological unification of experience — C.G. Jung *et al., Man and His Symbols,* pp. 200-11.

14. Teilhard, "Comment je crois," pp. 102-03.

15. Some 65 pages (137-203) of de Lubac's *Teilhard de Chardin* are devoted directly to the problems raised by this passage.

16. See his letter of March 1947, cited in de Lubac, *ibid.*, p. 187.

17. *Ibid.*, pp. 154–55.

18. Cf. *ibid.*, pp. 168 and 187. Although some of Teilhard's expressions are undoubtedly imprecise, de Lubac seems correct in insisting on the orthodoxy of their intent.

19. *Ibid.*, pp. 163–65.

20. Teilhard, "La Grande option" (1939); Eng. trans. in *The Future of Man,* pp. 45–47.

21. Teilhard, "Mon Univers" (1924), p. 66.

22. Rudolph Otto, *Mysticism East and West: A Comparative Analysis of the Nature of Mysticism,* trans. Bertha L. Bracey and Richenda C. Payne (New York: Collier Books, 1962), pp. 61–68.

23. Ramsey, *Religious Language*, p. 41.

24. Teilhard, "Le Paradoxe transformiste" (1925) Eng. trans. in *The Vision of the Past,* trans. J. M. Cohen (New York: Harper & Row, 1966), pp. 23–25.

25. Teilhard, "L'Histoire naturelle du monde" (1925); Eng. trans. *ibid.*, p. 104. Cf. Piet Smulders, S.J., *The Design of Teilhard de Chardin,* trans. Arthur Gibson (Westminster, Md.: Newman, 1967), pp. 31–32.

26. Georges Crespy, *From Science to Theology: The Evolutionary Design of Teilhard de Chardin,* trans. George H. Shriver (New York: Abingdon Press, 1968), p. 60.

27. Teilhard, "Le Paradoxe transformiste," p. 101; cf. *The Phenomenon of Man,* p. 218.

28. Wildiers, p. 56. Of course this analysis does not encompass the various non-European religious cultures.

29. Teilhard, "L'Histoire naturelle du monde," p. 104.   30. *Ibid.*

31. Teilhard, *The Phenomenon of Man,* p. 218.

32. Bernard Delfgaauw, *Evolution: The Theory of Teilhard de Chardin,* trans. Hubert Hoskins (New York: Harper & Row, 1969), pp. 105–06.

33. Teilhard, *The Phenomenon of Man,* p. 219; cf. "Comment je crois," p. 104.

34. Teilhard, *The Phenomenon of Man,* p. 41.   35. *Ibid.*, p. 43.

36. *Ibid.*, pp. 43–44.

37. Blaise Pascal, *Pensees,* trans. W. F. Trotter (New York: Dutton, 1958), n. 72, p. 17.

38. Teilhard, *The Phenomenon of Man,* pp. 44–45.

39. Teilhard, "Sur la Notion de transformation créatrice" (1920?); Eng. trans. in *Christianity and Evolution,* p. 22.

40. Coffy, p. 24. But certainly Rabut is right in noting that "as [Teilhard] himself says, he is more of a naturalist than a physicist, and it is impossible for a man to be a specialist in every field"—Rabut, pp. 20–21.

41. Cf. George Abell, *Exploration of the Universe* (New York: Holt, Rinehart & Winston, 1965), pp. 407–10.

42. Jastrow, p. 38; cf. p. 8.   43. *Ibid.*, p. 11; cf. p. 13.

44. *Ibid.*, p. 50.   45. Crespy, p. 42.

46. Teilhard, *The Phenomenon of Man,* p. 218.

116   *Christ and the Universe*

47. Teilhard, "Comment je crois," pp. 104–05. Cf. Wildiers, p. 55.

48. Cf. Olivier Rabut, O.P., *Teilhard de Chardin: A Critical Study* (New York: Sheed & Ward, 1961), pp. 25–26.

49. Jastrow, pp. 8–10.

50. Teilhard, "Comment je crois," p. 100. Otto too insists (p. 62) that the unity characterizing mystical vision has"scientific counterparts."

51. Teilhard, "L'Union créatrice," p. 174.

52. Teilhard, "Mon Univers" (1918), p. 277.

53. Teilhard, "Mon Univers" (1924), pp. 51–52.

54. Gray, p. 16.

55. Teilhard, "Comment je vois" (1948 – unpublished), p. 18.

56. Cf. Timothy Ware, *The Orthodox Church* (Baltimore: Penguin Books, 1963), pp. 216–23.

57. *Ibid.*, pp. 217–21. On the implications of this unification theme for spirituality, cf. *The Prayer of Jesus*, trans. a monk of the Western Church (New York: Desclée, 1967), p. 119.

58. Gray, p. 17.

59. See below, Chapter V, §2, for a fuller discussion of the influence of Christ as mediating archetype.

60. Teilhard, "L'Union créatrice," p. 174.

61. Teilhard, "La Lutte contre la multitude" (1917); Eng. trans. in *Writings in Time of War*, pp. 94–95. Teilhard recognized the technical problems of his philosophical formulations, but preferred to err, if need be, by excess rather than defect, if he might thereby provide a "pointer to truth" – see *The Making of a Mind*, p. 189. On the difficulties raised by this passage in particular, see Gray, pp. 21–25.

62. Gray, p. 28.

63. Cf. the editor's note in *Writings in Time of War*, p. 95, note 3.

64. Teilhard, "Mon Univers" (1924), p. 45.

65. Teilhard, "Comment je crois," pp. 129–30.

66. Teilhard, "Mon Univers" (1924), pp. 39–40.

67. Teilhard, "Vie et planètes" (1945); Eng. trans. in *The Future of Man*, p. 107.

68. Teilhard, *The Phenomenon of Man*, p. 146.

69. Cf., e.g., *ibid.*, pp. 141–46; and "Vie et planètes," pp. 105 – 10.

70. Teilhard, "Universalisation et union" (1942); Eng. trans. in *Man's Place in Nature*, trans. René Hague (New York: Harper & Row, 1966), p. 86.

71. Teilhard, "Vie et planètes," p. 106.

72. Cf. Smulders, p. 41; and George Gaylord Simpson, *This View of Life: The World of an Evolutionist* (New York: Harcourt, Brace & World, Harbinger Books, 1964), pp. 229–32.

73. Smulders, p. 42.   74. Gray, pp. 113, 117.

75. Teilhard, "L'Union créatrice," p. 174.

76. Teilhard, *Journal*, 11/10/17; unpublished, cited in Gray, p. 178, n. 23. Cf. "Mon Univers" (1918), p. 277.

CHAPTER FIVE

1. Teilhard himself follows the outline of creation, Incarnation, and Redemption to present the fullness of his Christological thought; cf. "Mon Univers" (1924), pp. 60–66.

2. Teilhard, letter of 1/26/36; Eng. trans. in *Letters to Léontine Zanta,* trans. Bernard Wall (New York: Harper & Row, 1969), p. 114.

3. Teilhard, letter of 12/13/18; Eng. trans. in *The Making of a Mind,* p. 268.

4. Michelangelo Allessandri, "Il pensiero di Pierre Teilhard de Chardin," *Divinitas* 3 (1959), p. 342.

5. Claude Tresmontant, *Pierre Teilhard de Chardin: His Thought,* trans. Salvator Attanasio (Baltimore: Helicon, 1959), p. 91.

6. Louis Cognet, *Le Père Teilhard de Chardin et la pensée contemporaine* (Paris: Flammarion, 1952), p. 146.

7. Gray, p. 24.   8. *Ibid.,* p. 25.   9. Cf. Rideau, p. 509.

10. Teilhard, "Note pour servir à l'évangelisation des temps nouveaux," p. 377.

11. Cf. Mooney, p. 174.

12. Teilhard, "Note sur les modes de l'action divine dans l'Univers," p. 32. Cf. Mooney, p. 175.

13. Cerfaux, p. 316.   14. *Ibid.,* pp. 322–23.   15. Huby, p. 40.

16. Maloney, pp. 102–06; 114–16; 122–23.

17. See Küng's discussion, with special attention to St. Thomas' *Summa Theologica,* in his study, *Justification: The Doctrine of Karl Barth and a Catholic Reflection,* trans. Thomas Collins (New York: Thomas Nelson & Sons, 1964), pp. 138–39. See also the colorful interchange between Teilhard and Allegra on this "myopia" in the theological tradition—Allegra, *passim,* but especially pp. 65–66 and 99.

18. Teilhard, "Mon Univers" (1924), p. 54.   19. *Ibid.,* p. 55.

20. *Ibid.,* pp. 56–57.   21. *Ibid.,* p. 79.

22. R. B. Smith, "The Place of Evil in a World of Evolution," *Teilhard Reassessed,* ed. Anthony Hanson (London: Darton, Longman & Todd, 1970), p. 67; cf. Mooney, pp. 168–81.

23. Teilhard, "Que-faut-il penser du transformisme?" (1930); Eng. trans. in *The Vision of the Past,* p. 154.

24. Teilhard, "Christologie et évolution," pp. 82–83.

25. Teilhard, "Le Dieu de l'évolution," p. 239.

26. Teilhard, "Introduction à la vie chrétienne" (1944), unpubl., p. 10; cited in Mooney, p. 162.

27. Mooney, p. 203. This Christological position is increasingly vindicated in modern theology; cf. Michael Schmaus, *Dogma: III. God and His Christ* (New York: Sheed & Ward, 1971), pp. 242–43.

28. René d'Ouince, S.J., Teilhard's friend and for many years his Provincial, made a special study of the theology manuals, showing their neglect of

Christ's role in creation—see his book, *Un Prophète en procès: Teilhard de Chardin* (Paris: Aubier, 1970), 2:39.

29. Teilhard, "Mon Univers" (1924), p. 81.

30. Teilhard, "Ce que le monde attend en ce moment de l'église de Dieu: Une généralisation et un approfondissement du sens de la croix" (1952), unpubl., p. 4; cited in Robert L. Faricy, S.J., "Teilhard de Chardin's Theology of Redemption," *Theological Studies* 27 (1966), p. 578.

31. Cf. Cuénot, pp. 61 ff., and Speaight, pp. 136 ff.

32. Teilhard, "Note sur le Christ universel" (1920); Eng. trans in *Science and Chris.*, pp. 16-17.

33. Gray, p. 12.   34. Teilhard, *The Divine Milieu*, p. 123.

35. *Ibid.*, p. 109. It is of more than passing interest to see a theologian of a quite different background and temperament take the identical approach: "If the whole cosmos was created in the image of the invisible God, in the First-born of creation, by him and for him, and if this latter resides in the world, through the Church of which he is the head, then the world is in the final analysis a 'body' of God, who represents and expresses himself in this body, in virtue of a principle of union that is not pantheistic but hypostatic"—Hans Urs von Balthasar, *Herrlichkeit: Eine theologische Asthetik* (Einsiedeln: Johannes Verlag, 1961), 1:653.

36. Mooney, p. 94.

37. Teilhard, "Introduction à la vie chrétienne," *loc. cit.;* cf. Mooney, p. 86.

38. Teilhard, "Mon Univers" (1924), p. 64.

39. Teilhard, "Le Prêtre," p. 209. Note the radical interpenetration of creation, Incarnation and Redemption.

40. Teilhard, *The Divine Milieu*, pp. 107-09.

41. Teilhard, "La Lutte contre la multitude," pp. 106-07.

42. Teilhard, "L'Union créatrice," p. 174. In his early period Teilhard posited a purely natural principle of unity—"omicron," a natural soul of the world, as it were, distinct from Christ-Omega. Cf., e.g., "L'Ame du monde" (1918); Eng. trans. in *Writings in Time of War*, pp. 177-90. But this dualism soon disappears, as Christ becomes for Teilhard the sole principle of unity and point of convergence for the universe.

43. Teilhard, *The Phenomenon of Man*, pp. 293-94.

44. Teilhard, "La Vie cosmique," p. 50.

45. Teilhard, "Le Prêtre," p. 207. Although the immediate context is eucharistic, Mooney rightly observes (p. 82): "Here Teilhard sees Christ prolonging the Incarnation when he descends to replace the bread and wine at Mass, but without restricting his action to the material species alone."

46. *Ibid.*, pp. 219-20.

47. Teilhard, "Super-humanité—Super-Christ—Super-Charité," pp. 165-66.

48. Teilhard and Blondel, *Correspondence*, p. 49.

49. Indeed, sometimes he is more cautious in the use of formal causality, as when he states that Christ acts as a "quasi-Soul" or "like a form"—"L'Élément universel," p. 299; "Forma Christi," p. 266.

50. Teilhard, "Forma Christi," p. 254.   51. *Ibid.,* p. 265, n. 13.

52. Cf. Iosephus Gredt, *Elementa Philosophiae Aristotelico-Thomisticae* (Romae: Herder, 1961), 1:181. But for the Platonic tendency to emphasize an intrinsic dimension to exemplarity causality, cf. Karl Rahner, S.J., *The Trinity,* trans. Joseph Donceel, S.J. (New York: Herder & Herder, 1970), p. 10, n. 5.

53. Teilhard, "L'Élément universel," p. 299.

54. J. S. Hickey, *Summula Philosophiae Scholasticae* (Dublini: M. H. Gill, 1953), 1:455, n. 2.

55. Teilhard, "Mon Univers" (1924), pp. 53-54.

56. Teilhard, "Forma Christi," p. 266.

57. Karl Rahner, S.J., *Theological Investigations,* trans. Cornelius Ernst, O.P. (London: Darton, Longman & Todd, 1961), 1:332, 330.

58. Teilhard, letter of 10/3/18; Eng. trans. in *The Making of a Mind,* p. 244.

59. Teilhard, "Forma Christi," p. 252.

60. Teilhard, "L'Esprit de la terre" (1931); Eng. trans. in *Human Energy,* p. 20.

61. See the passage from *The Divine Milieu* (pp. 59-60) cited in full above, p. 15.

62. Teilhard, *The Phenomenon of Man,* p. 36. Elsewhere, in view of possible higher life forms in the universe, Teilhard qualifies his affirmations regarding man.

63. *Ibid.,* p. 33.   64. Teilhard, *The Divine Milieu,* p. 60.

65. Teilhard, *The Phenomenon of Man,* p. 226.

66. Teilhard, letter of 8/7/23; Eng. trans. in *Letters to Léontine Zanta,* p. 54.

67. Teilhard, *Man's Place in Nature,* pp. 32, 36. Cf. "La Centrologie" (1944); Eng. trans. in *The Activation of Energy,* p. 110.

68. See the passage cited above, p. 4, from Teilhard, "En quoi consiste le corps humain," p. 13.

69. Teilhard, "Chute, Rédemption, et Géocentrie" (1920); Eng. trans. in *Christianity and Evolution,* pp. 42-43. Cf., on Bonaventure, Ewert H. Cousins, "The Coincidence of Opposites in the Christology of Saint Bonaventure," *Franciscan Studies* 28 (1968), p. 39.

70. I am indebted for this insight to Dr. Ewert Cousins.

71. Teilhard, *The Phenomenon of Man,* pp. 241-42, 244.

72. Teilhard, *Man's Place in Nature,* p. 99.

73. See the passage cited above (p. 85) from Teilhard, *The Phenomenon of Man,* pp. 293-94.

74. Cf. Teilhard, "En quoi consiste le corps humain?" pp. 12-13 (cited in part, above, p. 4).

75. Cf. Splett, p. 233, and above, Chapter I, the section on the Body as a model, pp. 3-6.

76. Teilhard, "La Messe sur le monde," pp. 36-37.

77. Mooney, p. 85.

78. Teilhard, "Quelques vues générales sur l'essence du Christianisme" (1939); Eng. trans. in *Christianity and Evolution*, p. 135.

79. Teilhard, "Réflexions sur le péché originel" (1947); Eng. trans. *ibid.,* p. 190.

80. Teilhard, "Le Christ évoluteur" (1942); Eng. trans. *ibid.,* p. 145.

81. *Ibid.,* p. 146. One of the esoteric issues posed by science today is that of the possibility of intelligent life on other planets. Many astronomers argue for the high statistical probability of such centers of life, although some eminent biologists, such as Simpson and Dobzhansky, insist there is a very low biological probability, given the radically "groping" character of evolution.

Teilhard felt keenly the significance of this issue and dealt with it in various essays. Because of his organic view of the Universe and of God's creative-salvific work, Teilhard could never accept the position advanced by some theologians that Christ would have absolutely no relevance for other worlds. Rather, Teilhard insists, the Universe in its organic unity must be bound together by one creation-salvation action. Granted this unity, one might wonder, however, if the Teilhardian position could not admit an encompassing action of the Word much more vastly mysterious than we can at the present imagine, one which would include many organically united facets—each a true key to the Whole, a gateway into the Plenum. In any case, it is Christ into whom earth's mankind is engrafted, and he represents for us the "genetic code," as it were, of the whole organism of creation.

82. Teilhard, "Un Seuil mental sous nos pas: du Cosmos à la Cosmogénèse" (1951); Eng. trans. in *Activation of Energy*, pp. 263-64.

83. Faricy, p. 575.

84. Teilhard, "La Lutte contre la multitude," p. 106.

85. Teilhard, "Un Seuil mental sous nos pas . . . ," p. 264.

86. Rideau, p. 172.   87. *Ibid.,* p. 548.   88. *Ibid.,* pp. 171-72.

89. Teilhard, *The Divine Milieu*, pp. 102-04.

90. Teilhard, "La Signification et la valeur constructrice de la souffrance" (1933); Eng. trans. in *Human Energy*, p. 52.

91. Speaight, p. 331.

92. Donald P. Gray, "Creative Union in Christ in the Thought of Teilhard de Chardin" (Ph.D. thesis, Department of Theology, Fordham University, 1968), pp. 288-89, 264-65.

93. Teilhard, "Mon Univers" (1924), pp. 63-64.   94. Mooney, p. 190.

95. Teilhard, "La Messe sur le monde," p. 33.

96. Teilhard, *The Divine Milieu*, pp. 82-83.

97. Teilhard, "Comment je vois," cited in Mooney, p. 170.

98. *Ibid.,* p. 19, n. 35.   99. *Ibid.,* p. 19.

INDEX OF NAMES

Note: To keep footnote references in these indices in their context, page numbers followed by *n* refer to main text pages where indicator numbers are found, rather than to the pages where the footnotes are actually printed.

INDEX OF SUBJECTS